The Story of The Lons
and the Lives of the People Who Lived There

Edited by Annette Rothwell

Team members:
Stephanie Bailey
Nicola Bennetts
Marlene Gallop
Mike Gates
Annette Rothwell
Mike Rothwell

Bitton Parish History Group

Published by Bitton Parish History Group
www.Bittonhistory.org.uk

Copyright Bitton Parish History Group
Bitton Parish History Group has asserted its right under the Copyright, Designs and Patents Act of 1988 to be identified as the author of this work.

All rights reserved. This book may not be reproduced or transmitted in any form without the prior written consent of the publisher, except by a reviewer who wished to quote brief passages in connection with a written review or broadcast.

978-1-716-25553-3
Imprint: Lulu.com

Bitton Parish History Group apologizes in advance for any copyrights that are in place of which it is unaware or which it has been unable to trace.

Foreword

Bristol has an acknowledged position as a centre for many things, among these, technological innovation: Brunel; commerce: the Merchant Venturers and the Slave Trade; civil unrest: the Bristol Riots; religious fervour: the Wesleys and Revival.

For the last 150 years, a rather fine country house in Bitton was home to a series of families whose lives reflect in some ways the vibrant life of the city itself. And so it was that The Lons attracted the attention of the Bitton Parish History Group, who decided to look into its diverse history.

Our investigation was led by Annette Rothwell, whose experience as an enthusiastic historical researcher gave us such valuable insights. Weekly episodes were sent to our membership. Those of us involved in the research found it fascinating, and it seemed that our members did too. It became apparent that a physical copy would prove popular, and we therefore decided to produce this book.

Many, including former residents of The Lons, generously gave time to provide us with information, photographs and interviews. Their contributions are acknowledged at the end of each chapter.

Bitton Parish History Group intends to continue research into projects of this kind.

Stephanie Bailey
Chair

The Lons - Timeline

Pre - 1868
- A field known as The Lons was exchanged by William Francis Cryer for some land belonging to James Frew Somerville.

1868-1895/7
- James Frew Sommerville had The Lons built as a comfortable and prestigious home for his family. Together with his father and brother, he ran the Bitton Paper Mill.

1897-1907/9
- Uriah Alsop, an innovative entrepreneur, who called himself a steam cabinet maker, built a successful furniture business in Broadmead.

1909-1926
- The stylish Edwardian Nicholetts family had a banker head of household and an Air Marshall son who was knighted and gained a long distance flying record.

1929-1931
- Charles Thornton Hall, his wife and son, spent two years developing the estate following a family tragedy.

1931-1946
- George Lancelot Wood, a prosperous undertaker and sculptor of marble and stone ran his business in Bristol from The Lons at the age of 71.

1948-1952
- Norman Hall and family - owners of Eezall a washing powder business

1953-1972
- Hugh Butler Folliott: Vermipeat compost manufactured in Saltford. His office was at The Lons, where his wife, Frances ran a school.

1974-1984
- The Lons Country Club: owned by Graham and Anne Miller, offering squash courts, a swimming pool, receptions and a nightclub.

1985-Current
- The building converted into a number of privately owned flats managed by The Lons Country Estate Management Company on behalf of the owners.

Contents

Chapter 1:	Introduction	1
Chapter 2	Ownership prior to 1868	3
Chapter 3	James Frew Sommerville	7
Chapter 4	Uriah Alsop	21
Chapter 5	The Nicholetts Family	33
Chapter 6	Charles Thornton Hall	51
Chapter 7	George Lancelot Wood	57
Chapter 8	Norman Hall and Eezall	75
Chapter 9	Hugh Butler Folliott	83
Chapter 10	The Lons Country Club	115

Chapter 1: Introduction

What do a plant pot maker, an undertaker, a wedding venue, a steam cabinet maker, a school, a paper mill manager, a long-distance flying record holder, washing powder and an Austrian governess have in common?

Some of us from Bitton Parish History Group discovered the links and more when, delving into census records, newspapers, electoral rolls and military records, we researched the history of the Lons and the people who lived there. We were excited to discover the stories from local people who knew some of the more recent inhabitants. Girls who had attended school at The Lons shared their memories with us and we enjoyed viewing wedding photographs taken at The Lons Country Club.

The Lons in the 1890s: photo courtesy of Bristol Records Office

We were amazed by some of our findings. We certainly hadn't been aware that Turkish Baths would have been an 1868 feature of the building, nor did we expect to discover that one of the children brought up there would come to have his portrait in The National Portrait Gallery. Entrepreneurship and sound business acumen enabled some inhabitants to afford the rent or purchase price – including the furniture maker with at least 24 children!

The Lons when a school: photo courtesy Bristol Records Office

Memories of life at The Lons are priceless. They include the story of a child refusing to wear a pig's head and photos of the school's theatrical productions and a squash game interrupted when Kingswood School was on fire.

Chapter 2   Ownership prior to 1868

It would appear that The Lons had been grass or pasture prior to James Frew Sommerville building it around 1868. There are no buildings on the land known as The Lons in this map dated 1842[1] from Ellacombe's *The History of the Parish of Bitton in the County of Gloucester*. Whilst there is some doubt as to the accuracy of the map – for example it shows the Midland Branch Railway which wasn't built until 1869; it is likely that it is the 1842 map with some additional detail added at a later stage [2] since Ellacombe's book was not printed until 1881. However, even with the discrepancies, there is no evidence of a building prior to the late 1860s.

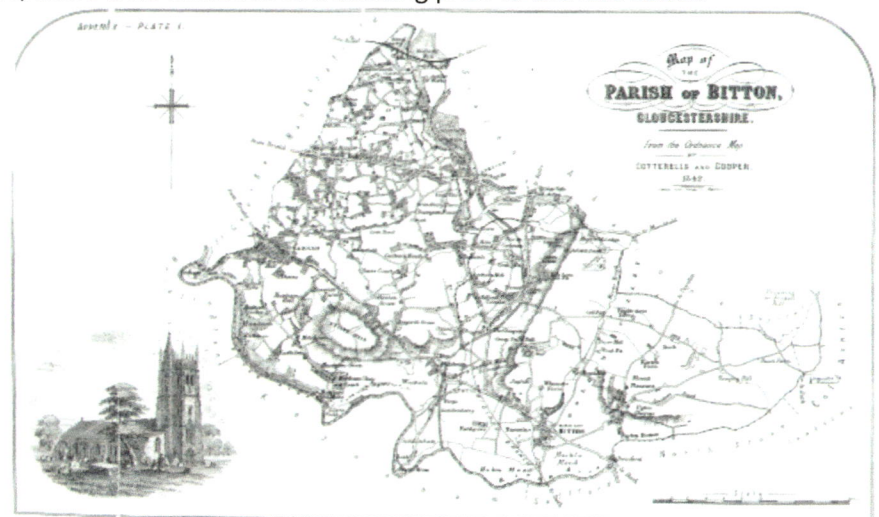

Plate I from The History of The Parish of Bitton in the County of Gloucester. Rev. H. T. Ellacombe M.A. F.S.A. Courtesy of Google Internet Archive[3]

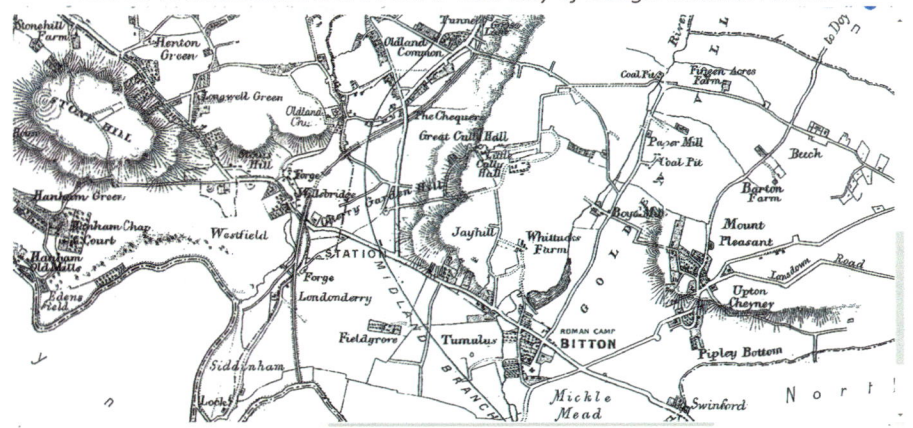

Enlarged section of Plate I from The History of The Parish of Bitton in the County of Gloucester. Rev. H. T. Ellacombe M.A. F.S.A. Courtesy of Google Internet Archive[4]

Immediately prior to 1868 the landowner was William Francis Cryer (1812-1870). William was a farmer and the 1851 census shows him to have 56 acres and be living in Upton. He is married to Mary Ann Crease. Ten years later his address is Knight's Folly Farm[5] in Bitton Village and he is farming 46 acres whilst employing two men and one boy.

The newspaper extract below gives notice of a land exchange. William swapped The Lons and a three-cornered paddock with part of Jay's Hill and a paddock belonging to James Frew Sommerville. This gave James Frew Sommerville the land he needed to build The Lons in 1868. William Cryer had previously been selling land. Two years earlier William had sold, at auction, land known as Hayne's or Pigeon House Leaze,[6] which lay on the west side of Oldland Common, adjoining Turnpike Road.

The Bristol Mercury, and Western Counties Advertiser, Saturday, April 25, 1868[7]

It would appear that William continued to live at Knight's Folly Farm, Bitton.[8] He died in 1870[9] and, a year later in 1871, the census shows his son, William Francis Cryer, to be living in Upton and farming 45 acres. Knight's Folly Farm was sold in 1877.[10] Today it is a camping site a little further down the road from The Lons. Whether Knight's Folly Farm and the farm in Upton where both father and son were said to live at various times is one and the same place is unknown.

[1] The History of the Parish of Bitton in the County of Gloucester by Rev H.T. Ellacombe
[2] https://www.brh.org.uk/site/articles/map-parish-bitton-1842/ accessed 16th October 2020
[3] The History of the Parish of Bitton in the County of Gloucester by Rev H.T. Ellacombe
[4] The History of the Parish of Bitton in the County of Gloucester by Rev H.T. Ellacombe
[5] 1861 England Wales and Scotland Census.
[6] Bristol Mercury 31st March 1866
[7] The Bristol Mercury and Western counties Advertiser, Saturday, April 25, 1868
[8] Gloucestershire Chronicle 22 April 1876
[9] England and Wales Government Probate Death Record
[10] The Field 16th June 1877 and Bath Chronicle and Weekly Gazette 28 July 1917

Chapter 3   James Frew Sommerville

Born on 4th April 1837, just two months before Queen Victoria came to the throne, James Frew Sommerville was in every sense a Victorian. As a paper maker he worked in one of the rapidly expanding industries of the era. As the owner of The Lons in Bitton he exemplified the successful head of a prosperous family; and the house and its grounds open a window on the lifestyle of a family of the burgeoning class of business owners.

James came from a paper making family. In 1835 his grandfather, William Sommerville, had started work to build the Dalmore paper mill on the River Esk at Auchindinny, just ten miles south of Edinburgh. The mill was up and running in 1837 the year that James was born. Three of William Sommerville's sons went into paper making. Hugh ran the Dalmore mill, Archibald ran a mill at nearby Lasswade, and, in 1849, William (James's father) came south and took on the mill at Bitton.

William Sommerville had married Isabella Frew at St Cuthbert's, Edinburgh, in 1834 and, by 1849, they already had a young family. Why did he and Isabella uproot and come such a long way from their home and wider family? The clue lies in reports in local and national papers of two fires in 1848 which caused catastrophic damage at the Bitton paper mill. In April 1849 the *Bristol Times* advertised the sale by auction of the paper machinery at Bitton.

Bristol Times and Bath Advocate, 7th April 1849.

The mill buildings might have needed rebuilding but the machinery was in situ and could be restored to working order. William would, presumably, have got quite a bargain and there would have been a number of skilled workers in the area keen to be re-employed.

The 1851 census confirms the date of the move. William is listed as a paper maker employing 146 workers, his age is given as forty-three, and Isabella's as thirty-six. They are living in Upton Cheyney with two daughters, Jane aged ten and Isabella aged seven, both of whom were born in Scotland. There is also a one-year-old son, Frank, but his birthplace is given as Keynsham. Subsequent censuses show that, as well as Frank and James, born in 1837, William and Isabella had three other sons: William, born in 1836, Alexander, born in 1839 and Robert born in 1852. They had two more daughters: Alice, born in 1855, and Lilias, born in 1857. Little Frank lived only to the age of six and their daughter, Isabella, died at the age of sixteen. Both children's deaths were remembered on the plate of their father's coffin when he died in 1899.

The Buckingham Chapel ©Matt Neale permission given by Bristol Tourist Information

The 1851 and 1861 census returns each include the name of a governess, presumably for the girls and the boys until they were old enough to go to school. James was fourteen when the family moved to Bitton but he and his brothers did not immediately join them. The 1851 census shows that they remained in Scotland at boarding school. In 1861 James, by now aged twenty-four, was living with his parents; his brother, William, appears as a visitor staying with the Spicer family in Hampshire. Spicers is a well-known name in the paper industry so perhaps William's was a work-related visit. Both William and James joined their father at Bitton Paper Mills and, in the 1871 census, James is described as a paper manufacturer. (The younger brothers, Alexander and Robert, also became paper makers running a mill at Creech St Michael, near Taunton.)

In 1865 James married Mary Gadd Matthews, the daughter of the late Thomas Gadd Matthews, a Bristol oil merchant. The wedding took place at the Buckingham chapel in Whiteladies Road, a non-conformist church built in Gothic revival style in the 1840s. Described as a 'fashionable wedding', it was a lavish affair reported in great detail in the *Daily Bristol Times and Mirror*. The bride, in a white satin dress and white tulle veil trimmed with Honiton lace, was attended by nine bridesmaids, her sisters and cousins and two of James's sisters, all in white and with different trimmings. The relatives and friends were 'conveyed to the chapel in sixteen coaches and pairs of greys, each of the coachmen wearing wedding favours'. After the ceremony the bridal party returned to the bride's home in Kingsdown Parade where 'a *recherche* breakfast had been prepared by Mr Nattrine of wine

Street'. When the happy couple left for London, en route for the continent, the remaining members of the party were taken to Mr Matthew's 'summer residence in Portishead'.

The Sommervilles, like the bridal family, were non-conformists. James and Mary's first child, Ernest Matthew Sommerville, born at Fair View, Keynsham Road, Willsbridge[1] on 27th September 1866, was baptised at the Congregational Church in St Phillips, Anvil Street, St Phillips. By the time the next son, James Frew Sommerville, was born on 27th May 1869 the family was living at the Lons. James was baptised at the (now demolished) Congregational Church in Cobden Street, Russell Town to which his grandfather, William Sommerville, was a generous donor when it was founded in 1868.

Three more children were born at The Lons: William Frew Sommerville (1872–1914), Isabella Mary Sommerville (1973–1953) and Ethel Martha Sommerville (1874–1962). Baptism records for these three have not yet been found; possibly they were baptised locally for various newspaper reports make it clear that James saw himself as part of the Oldland Common community. When, for example, he was urgently needed because there was a fire at the paper mill, a messenger was sent to Oldland Common where he was teaching at the Sunday School.[2]

Life at The Lons was comfortable. The house was newly built with 'ample kitchens and servants' quarters'. The 1871 census shows that Ernest and James had a live-in nurse and there was also a parlour maid and a cook. No doubt there were other servants who were not part of the permanent household. By 1881 the live-in help with the children had increased to an under nurse as well as a nurse and this was with Ernest and James away at boarding school! Both boys went to Barton Bank School in Hendon, London and it is, therefore, likely that William also went to Barton Bank although his birthdate means he escapes the census records which would support this. Ethel also attended boarding school but nearer to home. She was in Badminton House, part of a girls' boarding school situated opposite Bristol Zoo. Isabella may also have attended this school. In any case with servants, nurses and boarding school one can only imagine that time spent with parents would have been limited, as tended to be the custom in the late nineteenth century for children from a privileged background.

The Lons had extensive grounds which included two tennis courts. These were as much for fashion as for the benefits of physical exercise; particularly for women and girls, the game was not tennis as we know it today. Corsets, long skirts and hats (such as these advertised in the 1890s) restricted play to a gentle pat ball.

Both these advertisements appeared in many newspapers, local and national, in the 1890s

Inside the house the amenities included a Turkish bath. This was perhaps installed as a fashionable luxury or as an aid to good health – or both. Turkish baths were popular in the mid to late Victorian period with astonishing benefits trumpeted in the newspapers. An advertisement in the *Congleton Mercury* for 6 July 1870 is one of the more extravagant, claiming that a Turkish bath 'sweetens the temper, enlivens the disposition, invigorates the intellectual faculties, and sharpens the moral perception; it strengthens the muscular system, highly vitalises the blood and equalises the circulation, allowing of no stagnation anywhere'. It concludes with a lengthy doggerel in nine verses, one of which is enough to give a flavour of the whole:

> 'Visitors come with pain distracted,
> And some with limbs stiff and contracted;
> And home they go, their friends to tell
> The Turkish Bath has made them well.'[3]

Most Turkish baths were, however, in *public* places. There are also advertisements for thermal cabinets – a sort of Victorian version of flat-pack – but a letter of 1891 in the *Pall Mall Gazette* shows that having a properly installed Turkish bath in one's home was highly desirable, albeit unusual at the time:

'The ordinary bath of the household, now in such universal use as a health preserver, was, not many years back, a rarity...' Now, one sees every day advertisements of "Villa residences" at the modest rent of £30, with "bath-room fitted with hot and cold supply." Will not the still more potent remedial agent, hot air, be deemed an equal necessity of the future?'[4]

However fashion conscious they might have been, the Sommerville family took their position in society seriously with a paternalistic concern for the community. In 1860 *The Western Daily Press* reported on one in a series of lectures 'got-up by Messrs Sommerville of Bitton Paper Mills'. In the deferential tone of the period the newspaper article welcomed the lectures as a 'pleasing feature of the present time' and explained that they were 'for the mental improvement of the working classes'. The lecture in question was given by the local philanthropist, Henry Cossham, whose 'conversational style, graphic description of personal adventure, and the useful lessons deduced, afforded a rare treat'.[5]

In 1887, on the occasion of Queen Victoria's Golden Jubilee, the Sommervilles contributed to the day-long celebrations at Oldland Common, giving £5 for prizes and, in James's case, arranging for Bitton Paper Mills to provide material for flags and awning. The day's events were described in the *Bristol Mercury*:

> ...a church service (with an 'eloquent sermon'), a procession of children headed by the Warmley Tower brass band, a 'substantial' tea with 'a plentiful supply of ham and beef sandwiches being added to the usual afternoon fare', and finally sports which included a donkey race causing 'great amusement'.[6]

The Queen, The Lady's Newspaper
7th October 1899

The Sommervilles' largesse is an indication of the success of the Bitton Paper Mills. At the time of the 1891 census, they occupied three of the largest and most prestigious houses in the area: William (father) in Bitton Hill House overlooking the paper mill, William (son) at The Grange in Church Road and James at The Lons. The 1891 census records William Sommerville (Senior) as eighty-three and 'living on his own means'. His domestic servants include a nurse and his seventy-five-year-old wife, Isabella, is listed as being an imbecile. She was, presumably, suffering from what we should today recognise as Alzheimer's.

James's sons were by this time all working in the Bitton Paper Mill, Ernest as a clerk, James a carpenter's apprentice and William a millwright's apprentice. Home life continued to be comfortable for they remained at The Lons where there were four live-in servants: a cook, a kitchen maid, a parlour maid and a housemaid. Their apprenticeships in a business where they might have been expected to be managers suggest a serious attitude to their involvement.

The success of the business was not, however, without problems and setbacks, some of which were reported in the press. In 1868 they were charged with poisoning the water in the Boyd Brook and causing the fish to die.[7] In 1869 a twenty-two-year-old worker got his arm caught in machinery which tragically led to his death.[8] In 1876 there was a serious fire which the *Western Daily Press* reported would put the mill out of action for at least six months.[9]

As well as his work and his charitable activities, James was interested in politics and he took his civic duties seriously. He was on the board of St George's School. He was a member of the Liberal party and active in the Thornbury division of Gloucestershire. He was a member of the Gloucestershire County Council. His death on the eve of his being sworn in as a magistrate for Gloucestershire was unexpected even though he had been in poor health for some time. In its obituary on James Sommerville, the *Bristol Times and Mercury* reported that, before his death, he had spent a portion of the winter in Egypt.

> The funeral took place at Arno's Vale on Monday of Mr. James Frew Sommerville, whose death occurred somewhat unexpectedly on the previous Thursday at his residence, "The Lons," Bitton. The deceased gentleman was in his 58th year, and was on the eve of being sworn in as a magistrate for Gloucestershire. He was formerly a member of the County Council, and like his aged father, Mr. William Sommerville, J.P., who is still in a serious condition, he had identified himself in an active way with various Nonconformist movements. In business, he was associated with the Bitton Paper Mills.

Clifton and Redland Free Press, 22nd March 1895

> **OBITUARY.**
> **MR. J. F. SOMMERVILLE.**
> The death is announced, in his 58th year, of Mr. James Frew Sommerville, of The Lons, Bitton, a partner in the well-known firm of paper mill owners. The deceased gentleman had been in poor health for some considerable time, and passed a portion of the winter in Egypt. He was formerly a member of the Gloucestershire County Council, but retired three years ago, mainly on account of ill-health. So late as Monday week he was in business as usual, but he gradually got worse from that day, and died at an early hour yesterday morning. Mr. Sommerville displayed an active interest in local affairs, and it is a sad coincidence that his aged father has been lying seriously ill for several weeks.

The Bristol Times and Mercury, 15th March 1895

In 1895 life changed for the family with the death of James Frew Snr. It is in this year that Ernest left the family business and the partnership he had with W. and J. Sommerville at Golden Valley Paper Mills is shown to be dissolved on 1st July 1895.[10]

Ernest appears to have little more to do with the family from this time on and it is James, the second son, who has the responsibility of settling their father's GWR shares when he dies.[11] One can only speculate as to whether or not there was some kind of family dispute. There is also some doubt as to whether William even attended his father's funeral as his name is notably absent on the newspaper funeral accounts.

> NOTICE is hereby given that the Partnership heretofore subsisting between us the undersigned William Sommerville and Ernest Matthews Sommerville under the style or firm of W. and J. Sommerville at the Golden Valley Paper Mills Bitton has been dissolved by mutual consent as and from the 1st day of July 1895.—Dated this 27th day of July 1895.
> WILLIAM SOMMERVILLE.
> ERNEST MATTHEWS SOMMERVILLE.

London Gazette 30 July 1895

Nevertheless, Ernest is the first to leave his grandfather's business, he receives a much smaller amount than his siblings when his brother, William, dies[12] and, as will be seen, he also physically distances himself by emigrating to New Zealand.[13]

The Lons in 1890s
Photo courtesy of Bristol Records Office

The Lons was sold in 1896/7 so the family had to move elsewhere and, as will be seen, they did not all remain local to the area. By around 1900 the paper mill had been sold to the King Smith family and so all the male children were working elsewhere. Isabella and Ethel did not take part in paid work at any point in their lifetime, as was the custom with upper middle-class females of the time. Ethel lived on private means whilst Isabella was supported by her husband.

It is also likely that Isabella met her future husband whilst living at The Lons. In 1891 she was eighteen and a scholar. Lodging with Abraham and Elizabeth Haskins at Linden Lea, Oldland at this time was Vincent Milner (1866-1946) a physician and surgeon[14] who had recently qualified as a doctor in 1888.[15] In 1891 he unsuccessfully applied for the post of medical officer for Kingswood but continued to work in the area and conducted a number of post mortems – details of which are found in local newspapers. One can only imagine that Vincent and Isabella met during this time although when they married on 7th November 1900 Isabella had left Bitton and was living in Westminster.[16] Vincent had moved to Parkstone, Dorset probably around 1893-4 as he attended the Dorset and Hampshire BMA meetings at this time but was said to be from Kingswood. Following their marriage the couple lived at Oak Lodge, Poole Road, Parkstone, Dorset.[17]

Life for the children after they left The Lons
Ernest Matthews Sommerville

By 1901, having left the paper works, Ernest was in London, boarding at 100 Holland Road, Kensington[18] before moving to New Zealand later that year. Later that same year he married Margaret Mary Farraher in Sydney[19] and in 1905 the couple were living at Aorangi Terrace, Wellington North, New Zealand. Ernest was working as an importer. By 1911 the couple had moved to Aitken Street, Wellington North and they remained at that address until at least 1925. Ernest's mother died in 1904 and his brother, William in 1914. To date no evidence has been found of him returning to Britain at any time after his emigration but this does not mean he didn't do so.

By 1928 Ernest had retired and moved to 55 Palliser Road, Wellington East.[20] Five years later he died. There is some evidence (marriage record and family history) that he married Janet Kennie Millar Larkman (1892-1942) in 1933, but since he died in February of that year this may not be so.

Ernest died, aged 66, in New Zealand on 7th February 1933. The deceased estate record described him as an ex paper maker and importer formerly of Wellington who died intestate. He was buried in Totara Cemetery, Tauranga, Thames Valley, Bay of Plenty, New Zealand[21] and was noted as being a Presbyterian.

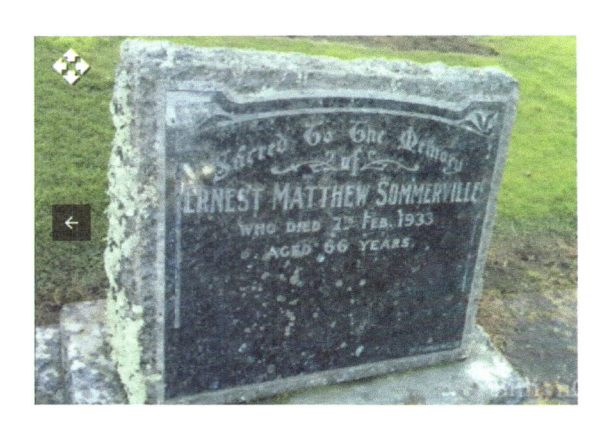

SOMMERVILLE Ernest Matthews of Tauranga **New Zealand** died 7 February 1933 Administration (limited) **London** 25 September to the honourable sir Thomas Mason Wilford K.C.M.G. attorney of the Public Trustee of New Zealand. Effects £516 8s. 4d. in England.

Janet Kennie Millar Larkman, Ernest's grave and probate:
photos courtesy of Wynne Family Tree on Library Edition of Ancestry

James Frew Sommerville

Following his father's death, it would seem that James was responsible for selling The Lons. At first he tried to rent it out but eventually he sold the house and land. By 1901 James had moved to Falfield and was boarding at Falfield Villa, Falfield, Thornbury[22]. He was living on his own means in the home of a widow, Bernice Isaac, and he appeared on the electoral roll in 1909 as renting a bedroom and sitting room from her. By 1913 he was renting from Mrs Isaac's son, E.O. Isaac and has two furnished rooms on the ground and first floor at The Laurels, Stone, Falfield.[23]

In 1904, whilst he was at Falfield, his mother died in Bournemouth and it was his sister, Isabella, who was the executor for her will. However, when his brother died in 1914 he was one of the executors on his will with his address as Stone, Falfield.

Shortly before the end of the war in 1918, aged 49, he signed attestation papers for the Royal Air Force[24] and gave his sister, Isabella, as the next of kin to be informed in the event of casualty. He was described as five feet ten inches tall with iron grey hair, brown eyes and a fresh complexion. He had a mole on his back and hammer toes on both feet. Medically he was a grade ii. He began as a learner petrol driver but maybe his learning wasn't that good as three months later he was remustered and became a general clerk. At discharge on 30th April 1920 his character was described as very good and his proficiency satisfactory.

James then moved to Dorset and from 1925 – 1939 was living at The Temperance Hotel, Blandford Forum[25], which later changed its name to Salisbury Hotel, on his own means.[26] There were a number of Temperance Hotels throughout the country. These operated in much the same way as any hotel except they did not serve any alcohol.

At some point James returned to Bath and he died in The Ear Nose and Throat Hospital Bath on 6th August 1948. His executor was his sister, Ethel who had returned to Bath some years before so it may be that he moved to Bath to be near her. His effects were £11,380.5s.11d. The Bath Chronicle and Weekly Gazette for 29th January 1949 provides an interesting account of how his estate was to be distributed.

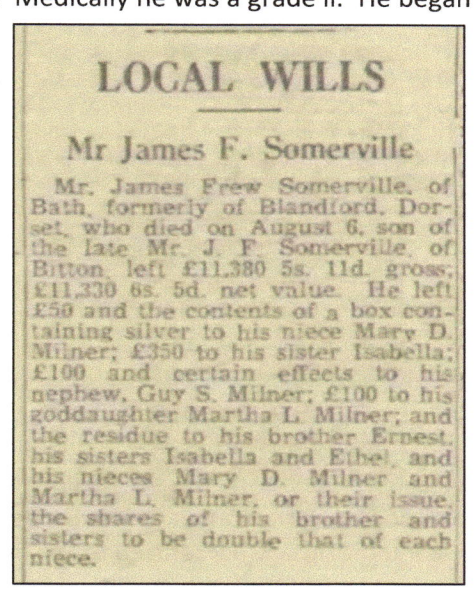

LOCAL WILLS

Mr James F. Somerville

Mr. James Frew Somerville, of Bath, formerly of Blandford, Dorset, who died on August 6, son of the late Mr. J. F. Somerville of Bitton, left £11,380 5s. 11d. gross; £11,230 6s. 5d. net value. He left £50 and the contents of a box containing silver to his niece Mary D. Milner; £350 to his sister Isabella; £100 and certain effects to his nephew, Guy S. Milner; £100 to his goddaughter Martha L. Milner; and the residue to his brother Ernest, his sisters Isabella and Ethel and his nieces Mary D. Milner and Martha L. Milner, or their issue, the shares of his brother and sisters to be double that of each niece.

Bath Chronicle and Weekly Gazette 29 January 1949

SOMMERVILLE James Frew of The Ear Nose and Throat Hospital **Bath** died 6 August 1948 Probate **Bristol** 6 December to Ethel Martha Sommerville spinster. Effects £11380 5s. 11d.

15

William Frew Sommerville

William appears to have left The Lons by the time of his father's death and there is some evidence that he may not have attended his father's funeral. Certainly newspaper accounts of the time do not list him as one of the mourners and the first carriage only contains his four siblings. In 1906 he was in the rate books as living in Portsmouth, Hampshire and in 1911 and 1913 his address was Lodge Hill, West Dean, Chichester. He was a farmer and his sister, Ethel was living with him as his servant.

> **MR. W. F. SOMMERVILLE.**
>
> Mr. William Frew Sommerville, of Nairobi, British East Africa, formerly of 23, Festing Grove, Southsea, and of Bitton, engineer, who was killed in action near Nairobi on the 25th of September last, aged 43 years, left unsettled property in the United Kingdom valued at £5,464 0s. 10d. Probate has been granted to his sister, Miss Ethel Martha Sommerville, of Bessingby Lodge, Parkstone, his brother, Mr. James Frew Sommerville, of Stone, Berkeley, Glos., and Mr. Frew Sparke Evans, tanner, of Trinmore, Clifton Down, Bristol. The testator left £1,500 each to his brother James Frew and his sister Isabella Mary, £250 to his brother Ernest Matthews, £100, his gold watch, and silver mug to his nephew Guy Sommerville Milner, and the residue of his property upon trust for his sister Ethel Martha for life, with remainder to her issue as she may appoint, or equally, and, failing issue, as she may otherwise appoint, and, failing such appointment, then equally between his brother James and his sister Isabella.

Clifton Society, 22 July 1915

It would seem that shortly after the census he travelled to Nairobi to work as a farmer since in August 1914 he joined the newly formed East Africa Mounted Rifles as a trooper. The unit was part of the East Africa Campaign which consisted of 400 volunteers who were expert riders, shot well and knew the country. Many also spoke Swahili. They had an unconventional attitude to warfare and apparently were taken aback when they discovered they were expected to wear uniforms. Most refused to live in barracks but stayed in nearby hotels or even in Government House. In addition, the soldiers were under equipped and short of supplies. Not only were they subject to attack by the Germans but were frequently victims of wild animals, disease and water shortages.

Trooper W. F. Sommerville, Nairobi British and Indian Memorial: Image courtesy of Find a Grave Indian Memorial Image courtesy of Find a Grave

William died on 25th September 1914. A lance corporal and six troopers, including him, were killed in action on that day so it is likely that there was some sort of skirmish. He is listed on the British and Indian memorial in Nairobi.

Isabella Mary Sommerville
Isabella lived with her husband Vincent Milner, physician and surgeon in Parkstone until they both retired.

In 1901 the couple had two servants, a cook and a housemaid and Isabella's sister Ethel was also living with them. They went on to have three children and by 1911 they also took on a nurse to help with the children. They took an interest in local life, winning a silver medal for best cat, Peter in the Parkstone and District Canine show in 1901 and Isabella was involved with local charity work including fund raising for a nursing fund.[27] In 1902 Vincent was appointed as medical officer in Parkstone and later became a Justice of the Peace, a town councillor and was on the school board.

On the death of her brother William in 1914, Isabella was left £1500 and her eldest child, Guy Sommerville Milner, was left £100, a gold watch and a silver mug. In 1925, eleven years after William's death, she applied for his medals.[28]

Vincent used his skills in the war effort and took paid employment with the Dorset 66, working as a surgeon at Cornelia Hospital, Poole in both the civilian and military wards.[29] By 1936 Vincent had retired and the couple moved to Torquay. To start with they lived at 6 Lower Terrace, Torquay, Devon but by 1939 they were living in a boarding house which appears to be for people living on private means and run by Alice and Arthur Edwards.[30]

During their retirement, between 1936 and 1939, the couple made annual trips to Villefranche, France[31] and it is likely that they also travelled to Italy since in 1939 their daughter, Lucy married an Australian in Milan.[32]

Ravenswood, Babbacombe Road, Torquay, an eight bedroomed guest house today
Photo courtesy Trip Adviser

Vincent moved into Mount Stuart Nursing Home where he died on 8th December 1946[33]. His daughter, Mary, was the executor with effects of almost £26,000. Isabella died seven years later on 24th December 1953 and was living in Hove. Probate was granted to her three children and her effects were just over £14,000.[34]

Ethel Martha Sommerville

Ethel left The Lons shortly after her father's death and moved in with her sister and husband at Oak Lodge.[35] She never married and throughout her life was described as living on private means.

By 1911 she had moved to Chichester and was living at Lodge Hill Farm with her brother, William.[36] When William moved to Nairobi she returned to Parkstone and lived at Bessingby Lodge. She was an executor on William's will in 1914 and after bequests was left his remaining property.

By 1925 Ethel had moved closer to the place of her birth and was living at 10, Cavendish Place, Bath when she and her nephew Guy Somerville Milner were executors for GWR shares following the death of Peter Frew Sparke Evans who died on board the ship, Arundel Castle, on 30th January 1925. She then moved to 58, Pulteney Street, Bath before moving back to Cavendish Place. By 1939 she had again moved and was living in Marlborough Buildings, Bath.[37]

Throughout her time in Bath she travelled abroad, visiting Madeira and Portugal.[38] This latter visit was in 1932 and she was accompanied by her niece, Mary Milner.

> SOMMERVILLE Ethel Martha of St. Marys Convent St. Aldhelms Road Branksome Park Poole spinster died 14 March 1962 Probate Winchester 24 May to Guy Minden Emerson solicitor. Effects £7620 19s. 6d.

Ethel died in 1962, aged 87, with the death registered in Poole Dorset.

Sommerville Way

The Sommerville family have dispersed but their name lives on in Bitton. Sommerville Way leads to the Linden homes built on the site of the Bitton Paper Mill.

[1] *Bristol Mercury* 28th October 1865
[2] *Bristol Mercury* 29th April 1876
[3] Free supplement to the *Congleton Mercury* 6th July 1870
[4] *Pall Mall Gazette*, 17th October 1891
[5] *The Western Daily Press,* 16th November 1860
[6] *The Bristol Mercury* 24th June 1887, p.3
[7] *The Bristol Mercury, and West Countries Advertiser,* 8th August 1868
[8] *The Western Daily Press,* 25th August 1869
[9] *Western Daily Press*, 25th April 1876
[10] *London Gazette* 30th July 1895
[11] Great Western Shareholders 1835-1932 for James Frew Sommerville 14 March 1895
[12] *Clifton Society* 22nd July 1915
[13] New Zealand, Electoral Rolls 1905, 1933 and numerous entries for intervening years
[14] 1891 census records for Oldland and Bitton
[15] Medical register for 1913 which shows that he had qualified in Edinburgh
[16] Marriage certificate for Church of St Andrew Parish of Westminster for November 7th 1900 and *Hampshire Advertiser* 14 November 1900
[17] 1901 census
[18] 1901 census
[19] New South Wales Marriages for 1901
[20] New Zealand Electoral Roll
[21] New Zealand Cemetery Records
[22] Electoral Roll for Parish of Falfield
[23] Electoral Roll for Parish of Ham and Stone
[24] Royal Air Force Service Record
[25] Electoral Roll for Blandford Forum
[26] 1939 register for Blandford Forum
[27] Bournemouth Guardian 25th July 1919
[28] W.F. Sommerville – East India Rifles Service Record
[29] Service record for Vincent Milner
[30] 1939 register
[31] Passenger lists leaving UK
[32] *Western Daily Press*, 2nd December 1939
[33] Government probate record
[34] Government probate record
[35] 1901 census
[36] 1911 census
[37] 1939 register
[38] Passenger lists leaving the UK

Chapter 4   Uriah Alsop

Following the death of James Frew Sommerville on 14th March 1895, newspapers[1] displayed adverts for the sale or renting of the Lons, furnished or unfurnished, one of which is shown below. It tells us about the class of person expected to be interested by emphasising the distance from wealthy Bath and Clifton (not Bristol) and its proximity to two major hunts.

However it did not appear to have been let or sold quickly, as the adverts continued until 10th September 1896, when Mrs Sommerville advertised the sale of the furniture at the house in the Bath Chronicle and Weekly Gazette. This is often a sign that the owner is moving house. Items for sale included furniture, carpets ('turkey, velvet pile and Brussels'), Grand and Cottage pianofortes, a billiard table, tables and chairs including ladies' chairs in silk and velvet, bedsteads and bedroom furniture, vintage wines, Madeira, port, brandy and rum from the cellar and outdoor equipment including a lawn mower.

DESIRABLE FURNISHED RESIDENCE to be LET.—"The Lons," Bitton, Gloucestershire, about six miles from Bath and a similar distance from Clifton, and about five minutes from Bitton Station. M. R., and 15 minutes' drive from Keynsham Station, G.W.R. This modern residence is handsomely furnished, with south aspect, commanding extensive views, and the accommodation comprises attractive entrance hall, dining and drawing rooms, and library, with ample kitchens and servants' offices on ground floor, while the bedroom accommodation, approached by two staircases, is ample for a gentleman's family. There is also a Turkish bath ; and the gardens and pleasure grounds, tennis grounds (two courts), and glass are in thorough order; and the stabling is excellent. Within reach of the Duke of Beaufort's and the Berkeley Hounds ; packs of harriers hunt the neighbourhood. Rent £200.—Apply to G. Bush and Bush, solicitors, 9, Bridge Street, Bristol.

Early advert describing the Lons
Army and Navy Gazette 8th June 1895

An ice cart:
Image courtesy canalmuseum.org.uk

Interestingly, the kitchen equipment included two refrigerators. As the property was never advertised as having an ice house, and the domestic refrigerator didn't start to appear in its present form for at least another 15 years, these were probably zinc-lined cupboards with ice trays. Ice would be delivered by 'ice cart' in blocks to local butchers and fishmongers, and perhaps to wealthier homes such as this.

But whatever furniture the next owners required would not have been a problem for them. Uriah Alsop was a wealthy furniture maker and house furnisher.

Uriah Alsop is first listed as a private resident at the Lons in 1897, with business address Broadmead Bristol,[2] and there was an advertisement for a general servant to join other servants at the Lons in

June 1897.[3] He probably purchased rather than rented the Lons, since it was occupied by the family until 1907, and then according to electoral registers[4] the freehold was held by two of the children, George Percy and Arthur Edward, and let out until at least 1915 and probably until 1927 when the next occupiers, the Nicholetts, left.

Who was living in the house during this time? We know that in 1901 the occupants were Uriah (71), a house furnisher and head of the household, and his wife Selina (57), together with their five unmarried children, James Herbert (27) also a house furnisher, Charles (25) a professional organist, Arthur Edward (23) a cashier in the furniture business, Cornelia Beatrice (20), and George Percy (18) a cabinet maker. Uriah's widowed sister Angelina Lewis (57) was the housekeeper. All were born in Bristol. There were three further servants, Bristol born Bridget O'Bryan (57) the cook, and sisters from Batheaston, Emma Jones (30) a housemaid and Louisa Jones (26) a general servant. As only Uriah was given as being an employer, he was at least nominally running the business.

There was one other person who we know lived at the Lons during the Alsops' occupancy, a young servant called Caroline Windsor, who was caught stealing by Angelina and charged on 4th August 1899.[5]

> A SERVANT IN TROUBLE.
> Caroline Windsor, 15, was charged with stealing 14 books, nine silver bangles, one silver pencil case, one brush, and four handkerchiefs, of the value of 15s, the property of Uriah Alsop, of the Lons, Bitton. The prosecutor identified the articles as his. The housekeeper at the Lons said that being suspicious she examined the defendant's box in her bedroom, where the various articles were found. Windsor was a servant under her charge. The case was adjourned for a week.

Bristol Mercury 4th August 1899

As Caroline's behaviour was described as 'good' whilst on remand, she was released with a fine of 2s.6d. a week later.

The Alsops appeared to be a typical, well to do family. Uriah was a very successful entrepreneur, but he'd had a rather colourful private life.

Uriah Alsop was baptised on 22nd February 1829 at St. Philip and St. Jacob, Bristol. His father, also called Uriah Alsop, was a clock maker, and his mother Mary Ann (née Slocombe) was the daughter of a carpenter. He would thus, no doubt, have gained knowledge growing up about both carpentry and clock cabinet making.

He was brought up in central Bristol, living in Milk St., St. Paul, and in 1850 he married 19-year-old Ann Naish, the daughter of Henry Naish, the Parish Clerk of St. Pauls and St. Philips. The following year he and Ann were living next door to his in-laws in Jacob Street. He was a cabinet maker. Ten years later his business was beginning to prosper and he was living at 1 St James Barton with wife Ann, two children and three servants. He was still a cabinet maker, but now employed 28 men and 2 boys. By 1871 he and his family had moved up in the world again and were living at Limetree House, St. James Barton. He described himself as a cabinet manufacturer and his workforce had grown to 84 men and 2 boys.

A house possibly like Limetree in St James Barton, prior to demolition in the 1950s

Ten years later and he and Ann, five of their children and two servants were living in the wealthy area of Clifton at Alma House, 25 Alma Road. Uriah had become a Town Councillor and his booming business now employed 136 men and 8 boys. By this time, he and Ann had produced 18 children.

However, by 1891 Ann and Uriah are living apart following Ann's unsuccessful attempt in 1889 to divorce Uriah on the grounds of his 'incestuous' relationship with her *sister* Selina, 12 years her junior. But Uriah had contested that it was incestuous, and the divorce case was stayed[6].

Alma House: Image courtesy Zoopla

Divorces then were very expensive and therefore uncommon. Only a very small proportion of these petitions arose where a woman brought divorce proceedings against her husband and very few of those were subsequently granted in the woman's favour. Given all that, this was still perhaps a surprising result, as it was deemed to be incestuous under the Marriage Act of 1835 to *marry* the sister of your *dead* wife (this wasn't repealed until the 1907 Deceased Wife's Sister's Marriage Act), so Ann would certainly be holding the moral high ground. Whether some financial arrangement with Ann had been agreed as settlement, we know not.

Ann was now living at 53 Cotham Road with four of her children and one servant. Her son Uriah Henry was a wholesale cabinet maker. Ann, rather unusually, stated on the census that she was married, but 'living apart from my husband'.

At the same time Uriah and Selina were visiting Tottenham where Clara Ann Slocombe (Alsop), the eldest daughter of Uriah and Ann, was living with her husband Henry Watkins, a clerk. Uriah and Selina both stated that they were 'married'. Uriah was curiously listed as a Manchester manufacturer (cotton). However, Ann's children have clearly not completely ostracised him. Furthermore, Augusta Maude Alsop, another of Uriah and Ann's children, and four of Uriah and Selina's children were actually now living at Alma House with Uriah's mother. It is stated that these children were living with their father, a cabinet maker. Therefore one can infer that Uriah and Selina were also living there and that Ann had moved out of the matrimonial home, voluntarily or otherwise. The fact that Ann is living on her own means suggests that a monetary settlement may have been made.

In fact, Uriah and Selina were living with five of *their* children at the Lons. We know this because all five, along with their other son Walter William Naish Alsop, were baptised (with Uriah and Selina named as parents) at Whitchurch, St. Nicholas, during 1892. And it is two of *their* children who would be executors on Uriah's will – Walter William Naish Alsop and Arthur Edward Goodier Naish Alsop. One might infer that Uriah had trusted these two to carry out his wishes more than, for instance, his and Ann's (Uriah) Henry Alsop, even though Henry was a 'governor' in the company from 1891[7] and inherited the manufacturing business when Uriah died.[8]

Ann was now 'living on her own means' in Hornsey, Middlesex with one servant. She was being visited by her and Uriah's youngest son Stuart James Alsop, a clerk (employer), who lived nearby.

Uriah had been very involved in society in Bristol, among other things as a member of the first School Board in Bristol, representing Clifton Ward in the City Council from 1880 to 1886,[9] president of the Working Men's Conservative Association[10] and also chairman of the Bristol Cooperative Land and Building Society.[11]

We do not know why Uriah and Selina had moved out of central Bristol to the rural village of Bitton. It may have been to avoid any societal scandal, but they may just have wanted a quieter life in Uriah's later years. Uriah and his sons could easily run the business by travelling to central Bristol by train from Bitton station.

The family do not seem to have partaken in many local functions whilst at the Lons. Some of the children did become involved with the Bitton Flower Show run by the Bitton and Oldland Common Horticultural Association. This had taken place annually from 1890 on the field next to Bitton station and had about a thousand entries each year. There were various classes of non-horticultural items too, including poultry, pigeons, butter, cream and honey. At the ninth annual show,[12] the Association's committee included James and Arthur Alsop, and James won second prize in one of the pigeon classes. In the 1905 show,[13] Arthur Edward, James and George were all named as being on the committee.

In 1898 Arthur Edward and James played for Bitton Cricket Club. Both batted and scored 0![14] A year later the 12th Annual meeting of the Bitton and Oldland Cricket Club took place at its 'headquarters', the White Hart Hotel, and Uriah and James were named as patrons, with James also a committee member.[15]

At another event on the field next to Bitton Station, a Fancy Fair and Fete for 'parochial needs at Oldland' was held on the 8th July 1905. Among the notables present were the High Sheriff of Bristol and a 'Mrs U. Alsop', i.e. Selina.[16]

Uriah died aged 77 on February 18th 1906. His funeral cortege left from the Lons[17] and was a huge affair.[18]

THE LATE MR URIAH ALSOP.—Mr Uriah Alsop's funeral will leave his residence, The Lons, Bitton, on Saturday next, at 9 a.m., expecting to arrive at Arno's Vale Cemetery at 11.30 a.m. The coffin is made of mahogany, at the express wish of the deceased. The establishments at Broadmead, Fairfax Street, and 47, Lower Union Street will be closed all day. The office staff and assistants with the whole of the employés, will meet the cortege at the top of Brislington Hill, and will join in the procession to the cemetery. The office staff and assistants are sending a wreath, as also are the employés.

Western Daily Press 22 Feb 1906

FUNERAL OF THE LATE MR URIAH ALSOP.—The funeral of the late Mr Uriah Alsop took place on Saturday. The cortege left the deceased gentleman's residence at Bitton about ten o'clock, and at Brislington it was met by the employés, who numbered about two hundred. The service was conducted at Arno's Vale Cemetery by the Rev. A. W. Riley, and among those present, in addition to members of the family, were Mr R. W. Nurse (Willsbridge), Mr C. E. Barry (solicitor), Mr E. Kidd, Mr W. C. Farbrother (cashier), representing the office staff and wholesale departments; Mr F. Flexney, representing the retail department; and Mr J. H. Powell, representing 47, Lower Union Street. The pall-bearers, who consisted of the oldest workmen in the employ of the firm, were Messrs G. Davidge, A. Garland, F. Parsons, C. Harris, G. Coggins, C. Green, and W. Tovey, the oldest employé. The body, which was enclosed in a mahogany casket, was placed in a vault. The complete arrangements for the funeral were carried out by Messrs Lewis and Son, Stokes Croft.

Western Daily Press 26th February

His probate was published in the local papers:[19] Mr. Uriah Alsop, of the Lons, Bitton, and Bristol merchant and cabinet manufacturer, who died on February 18th, left estate valued by the Rev. Walter William Naish Alsop, of Ivy Villa, St. Andrews Road, Barking, and Arthur Edward Goodier Naish Alsop, of the Lons, at £32,274 of which £10,810 is net personalty.

Selina died at the Lons on the 1st August 1907. Her will was registered in the name of **Miss** Selina Naish Alsop.[20] Uriah's wife Ann Alsop died on 25th August 1906.

Uriah Alsop was clearly of some standing in the Bristol locality. He even had a road named after him – a sign that he is a person of some prestige.

Alsop Road in Kingswood is believed to have been named after 'Uriah Alsop of Bitton, steam cabinet maker', according to Veronica Smith in *Street Names of Bristol*.

Uriah Alsop's Furniture Business

Uriah Alsop's marriage to Ann Naish in 1850 had cemented him into the more middling classes from his tradesman background, his business as a cabinet maker starting in Broadmead in about 1849.[21] In an indenture of 1859, he is described as a timber merchant and cabinet maker.[22] 'Cabinet making' required the highest end of furniture making skills, but could also include furniture making as a whole, including chairs:

Left image: A Windsor chair from ~1850 stamped 'Uriah Alsop'[23]

Right image: a two-man saw in operation[24]

Furniture production may not be the first industry which one thinks of when it comes to the application of mass production methods. Certainly up until the late nineteenth century the vast majority of furniture items were made in small workshops, with skilled use of hand tools and much hard physical work.[25] Even the wood required was from logs sawn into planks using two-man saws. (A tree log would be placed over a deep pit, with one man staying above the pit and the other man getting into the bottom of the pit. A two-handed saw was used to saw the log into planks. Due to the sawdust produced the man at the bottom was called the 'under dog', whilst the one above was called the 'top dog').[26] But as the country's population had grown rapidly from the end of the eighteenth century, and through the first half of the nineteenth century, so did the demand for furniture.

Growing up, Uriah may have been inspired by the power of steam shown in 1840 by the GWR trains running from the newly opened Bristol Temple Meads station and by the launching in the floating harbour of the steamship SS Great Britain in 1843. He may well also have seen steam power used in industry, and in sawmills on his timber buying journeys. He often called himself a 'steam cabinet maker'.

Image left: A Firefly class broad gauge locomotive introduced by GWR between 1840 and 1842[27]
Image right: Launch of SS Great Britain[28] (courtesy Wikipedia)

Uriah was probably one of the earliest furniture makers to use steam powered machinery throughout the manufacturing process. In January 1857 we know that he was using a steam-powered sawmill, as a newspaper report[29] described a fire gutting his premises at the back of Broadmead and Union Street, the origin of the fire being the boiler of a steam engine powering a sawmill. Uriah stated that he wasn't insured, as the insurance company wouldn't grant him insurance because of the steam-engine! But on January 31st another newspaper report[30] quoted him as saying that he had acquired alternative arrangements at eligible workshops at number 18 Broadmead for existing orders to be fulfilled.

He was not deterred in using steam for long, as an 1883 document, 'Work in Bristol – A Series of Sketches of the Manufactories in the City' produced by the *The Bristol Times and Mirror* gave an extensive history of 'Mr. Uriah Alsop's Steam Cabinet Works.'[31] The publication, written by a reporter but no doubt guided by Uriah, claimed that from 1863 or earlier Uriah was utilising steam power to produce cheaper and often better quality furniture, saving much long, hard and expensive manual work. When he gradually introduced machinery it reduced the workload of his workmen, but increased their earnings. He was decried by others in the trade who said he would ruin the cabinet making business. But he had proved them wrong. By 1883 he was opening his huge premises every Wednesday for visitors to come and 'be astonished at the speedy and effective manner in which the various parts of chairs, sofas etc are turned, shaped and fitted'. There were machines, driven by a 50 horse-power steam engine, for virtually every stage of furniture making, and vast stocks of wood and veneers from all over the world. He didn't only make furniture by this time either, importing feathers, flocks, wool, millpuff etc, which he sold separately, and also to make bolsters, pillows and mattresses in the manufacture of his beds (both wood and iron). He sold carpets and hangings, so that overall he could 'completely furnish the largest mansion or the smallest cottage'. Finished items were sent locally and to all parts of the world, but mainly to the north and west of England, despatched in horse drawn carriages, by rail and by water.

Grand opening of the Clifton Suspension Bridge: Source: Wikipedia – Anon, accessed 20 Oct 2020

The premises were described as 4 or 5 story buildings with extensive frontage on Broadmead and Fairfax Street, and with 300 windows, 700 feet of steam pipe (also used to heat the buildings) and 800 feet of gas pipe spread over the various departments. He had obviously learnt from previous experience, as the buildings had concrete floors and sliding iron doors to isolate areas in the event of fire. There were even toilets in each department for the workers.

He appeared to have been a generous employer for the time, with newspaper accounts of a large pay rise for his workers[32] and huge works outings involving all of his employees. One notable account is given when 100 of his workers joined the grand parade holding models of the company's furniture at the grand opening of the Clifton Suspension Bridge on 8th December 1864,[33] which was followed later in the day by Uriah treating his workers to a gala party.[34]

> 'Mr Uriah Alsop, steam cabinet works, Broadmead, gave a splendid dinner to the whole of the workforce in his employ, when upwards of 150 sat down to the dinner, supplied by Mr. W. Hatton. It was served up in one of the large warerooms of the factory, which had been nicely fitted up with banners, evergreens, flowers, mottoes etc. Mr. Alsop presided... the Bristol and Gloucestershire brass band played some very appropriate airs during the evening'

So we can see that Uriah Alsop was an important Bristol businessman and entrepreneur, who had introduced steam powered mechanised production methods to make furniture in Bristol. Indeed, by the time that he came to The Lons, his company owned shops at 57, 58, and 59 Broadmead with manufactories in Fairfax Street and Union Street, and was reported to be one of the largest furniture manufacturers in the Kingdom. His company employed hundreds of men and boys:

'Manufacturing Furniture by Steam Power – Mr Alsop's Cabinet Works, situate at Broadmead, Bristol is thus spoken of by one of the leading Bristol Papers: Long before this addition was made, Alsop's Cabinet Works had obtained more than a national reputation. For a long time it has been an admitted fact the firm is by far the largest in the United Kingdom, and the export trade is simply enormous….we have no wish to exaggerate, because our readers are invited to visit the works, when they can see for themselves the immense quantities of manufactured goods stored, not only in the large and imposing front shop facing the Broadmead, which, fine as it is, can only be said to be a most diminutive representative of such a colossal establishment. The new department is devoted entirely to the display of the highest class of furniture and decorative work.' Bristol Times and Mirror[35]

'Mr U Alsop's Cabinet Manufactory – No more reliable evidence could be afforded that a business is prosperous than the fact that it is constantly out-growing the limits of the premises in which it is conducted and the frequent extensions which Mr Uriah Alsop has been obliged from time to time to make.. shows not only the rapid growth of business but also marks the development of a trade which... is becoming one of the staple industries of Bristol, the dealers of the north, the west, the west Midlands and South Wales now accustomed to resort to Bristol for their supplies. Few people viewing the front elevation of Mr Alsop's premises in Broadmead would imagine that stretching away to the rear as far as Fairfax street, a distance of 380 feet, and a breadth of 95 feet at its greatest width, was a vast range of workshops, showrooms and stores, in which about 300 people were employed, producing some of the most costly and artistic furniture that the refined tastes what in furnishing terms has been termed an aesthetic age could suggest, and producing with the aid of steam power beautiful cabinets, over mantels and those other devices of the cabinet maker's art in Chippendale, Queen Anne and other patterns…the demand for increased showroom accommodation has led to further extension of the premises which has just been completed.'[36]

After Uriah died in 1906 (Uriah) Henry Alsop inherited the manufacturing business and in 1911 was living at Rodney Hall, Filton. In an advert in 1909 Henry was the sole proprietor of the 'original and old-established firm for well made furniture' of Alsop and Son of 11, Castle Street, Bristol. It stated that the company had been established for 60 years.[37] James, Arthur and George Naish Alsop also continued to be occupied in the furniture business in Bristol. Although Charles' occupation was 'professional organist' in 1901, in 1919 he at least briefly had a furniture shop in the name of Charles Alsop and Son, at 215 Gloucester Road, Bristol.[38]

'Alsop's' was still advertising until 1939,[39] but did not appear again after the war. These photographs of Alsop furniture shops in Union Street were taken in the 1920s or 1930s.[40]

Union Street, 1920s or 30s: Images courtesy Keynsham and Saltford Local History Society

Uriah Alsop was a great self-publicist and knew the power of newspapers both in advertising his business and the man himself, as this article of 24th March 1945[41] illustrated:

> 'To this school of old-time business men Uriah Alsop belonged. He was a prolific advertiser in our columns and... recognised and supported the Western Daily Press almost from the first issue in June 1858. ...he wore sombre clothes and side whiskers and is well remembered.'

---

[1] Bath Chronicle and Weekly Gazette 2nd April 1896 and 23rd July 1896
[2] 1897 Kelly's Directory of Gloucestershire
[3] Wiltshire Times and Trowbridge Advertiser 12th June 1897
[4] Southern or Thornbury 1915 Bitton Ownership Voters The Lons Arthur Edward Alsop and George Percy Alsop
[5] Bristol Mercury 4th August 1899
[6] Ancestry.co.uk England and Wales Civil Divorce Records 1858-1918 1889 Wife's Petition, Divorce Court File No. 3329
[7] Wells Journal 27th August 1891
[8] Bristol Morning post 20 April 1906
[9] The Clifton and Redland Free Press 23 February 1906
[10] Western Daily Press 6 October 1880
[11] Western Daily Press 29 August 1877
[12] Bristol Mercury 21st August 1899
[13] Western Daily Press of the 21st August
[14] Bristol Mercury 1st July 1898
[15] the Bristol Mercury of 24th February 1899

[16] Western Daily Press 8th July 1905
[17] Western Daily Press 22 Feb 1906
[18] Western Daily Press 26th February 1906
[19] Gloucester Citizen 19th April 1906
[20] Gloucester Citizen 3/8/1907
[21] Bristol Mercury 7th August states 1899 is 50th anniversary
[22] London Gazette 4th October 1859
[23] http://www.nationaltrustcollections.org.uk/object/253288.1
[24] Image courtesy Wikipedia https://en.wikipedia.org/wiki/Whipsaw Latrobe Photographic Collection, National Trust Tasmania
[25] For further reading re London furniture making: https://historicengland.org.uk/images-books/publications/behind-the-veneer-south-shoreditch/
and also https://qmro.qmul.ac.uk/xmlui/handle/123456789/1472 then KIRKHAMFurniture-Making1982.pdf
[26] Vernacular craft to machine assisted industry (copyright Loughborough University):https://repository.lboro.ac.uk/articles/Vernacular_craft_to_machine_assisted_industry_the_division_of_labour_and_the_development_of_machine_use_in_vernacular_chair-making_in_High_Wycombe_1870-1920/9332600
[27] Courtesy Wikipedia origin unknown
[28] Picture is the copyright of the Lordprice Collection and is reproduced on Wikipedia with their permission. This work is free and may be used by anyone for any purpose
[29] Bristol Mercury 24 January 1857
[30] Bristol Mercury 31 January 1857
[31] Bristol Industrial Archaeological Society - Work in Bristol 1883 b-i-a-s.org.uk, copied from the Bristol Reference Library
[32] Bristol Mercury 9 December 1865
[33] Western Daily Press 9 December 1864
[34] Western Daily Press 9 December 1864
[35] South Wales Daily News Cardiff, Glamorgan, Wales 8 July 1884
[36] Western Daily Press 26 November 1885
[37] South Bristol Free Press and Bedminster, Knowle and Brislington Record 11 December 1909
[38] South Bristol Free Press and Bedminster, Knowle & Brislington Record Saturday 05 April 1919
[39] Bristol Evening Post 22 June 1939
[40] Image courtesy of Keynsham and Saltford Local History Society
[41] Western Daily Press 24 March 1945

Chapter 5   The Nicholetts Family

The Lons had been advertised for auction several times in 1906 and 1907, but it appears that it was not sold[1] and two of the Alsop brothers retained a share in the freehold of The Lons until at least 1915.[2] The Nicholetts family moved into The Lons around 1909 and so would have been renting the property from Uriah Alsop's children, at least in the initial years, but probably until they left around seventeen years later since after they leave, the for sale advert states 'By direction of Joint Vendors'[3] which suggests there was more than one seller, the Alsop children. The Nicholetts are found to be living at The Lons on the electoral roll from 1912 until 1925,[4] on the 1911 census and in a number of Kelly's Directories from 1909 onwards.

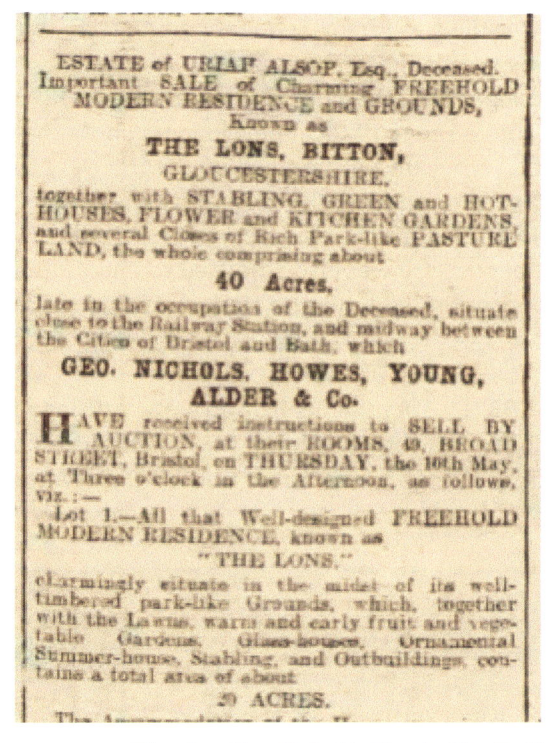

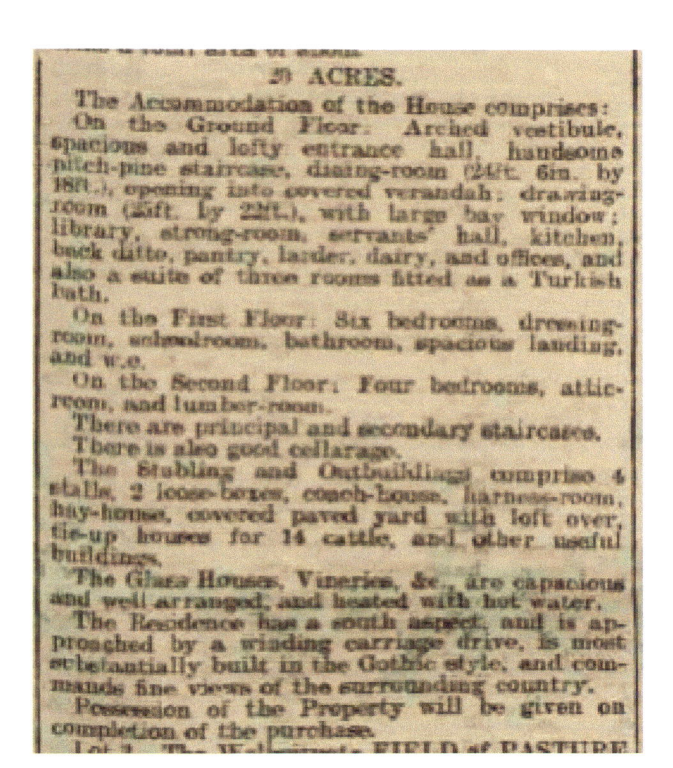

The Auction Sale Notice in the Bath Chronicle and Weekly Gazette 26 April 1906

The Nicholetts were buying into a stylish lifestyle with lots of modern conveniences, shown by the detailed sales and auction descriptions of The Lons above. The house offered them all the trappings which a fashionable upper class Edwardian family could expect.[5] As we will see, the family was both financially successful and used to a lavish lifestyle. Edward Nicholetts and his wife, Ellen, played a full part in local events and were involved with several charities. Edward worked in senior positions at Stuckey's bank in Bristol, amongst others. Later, their children also took part in community life. The couple had two daughters and a son living with them at The Lons. This latter had a celebrated life and can be considered as one of Bitton's alumni. Amongst his achievements which we will look at later are: a highly successful career in the RAF; survival from a plane crash gaining nationwide publicity; a world record for long distance flying; heroism in WW2 when fighting the Japanese before being captured as a Japanese prisoner of war.[6] He achieved top positions in the RAF and was knighted. His picture hangs in the National Portrait Gallery.[7]

So who were this fashionable young family who moved to The Lons around 1909?

Born March 14th 1864 in South Petherton, Devon,[8] Edward Nicholetts (1864-1954) came from a family of solicitors which included his father and both grandfathers, although his father later went into banking.[9] Edward was named after his uncle, who died at Rugby School aged just 16, five years before he was born.[10] His mother, Blanche, was the daughter of Sir A. W. Chichester, 7th Baronet of Raleigh, Devon.[11] Edward attended Eton College[12] and then became a banker. By 1893 he was joint manager of Stuckey's Bank in Tiverton[13] and a range of local newspapers show that he played a prominent role in local life. For example, he became a member of the 3rd Devons Volunteer Battalion – a Special Reserve group of civilians who undertook regular training to keep them fully prepared to join the army in the event of war or national emergency – he became a supernumerary Captain and Honorary Major of the Battalion.[14] He was also admitted to The United Grand Lodge of England Freemasons.[15] These interests continued when he took up residence at The Lons.

In 1899 Edward married Ellen Fanny Hollond (1872-1932). Ellen came from a very privileged background. She was the daughter of John Robert Hollond, a former Liberal MP for Brighton, a barrister, Justice of the Peace, HM Lieutenant for the City of London, director of Colne Valley Water Company[16] and celebrated hunting enthusiast.[17]

Wonham House, Bampton, Devon. The house and grounds; the entrance hall. Ellen's family home where she was living prior to her marriage to Edward Cornewall Nicholetts.[18]

The 1891 census shows the family to be living at Wonham house, Bampton. Ellen has brothers at Harrow School and Cambridge University. The family have thirteen live in servants including a butler, two footmen, six housemaids, a housekeeper, a lady's maid and nurses - surely a lot of servants even for 1891! Ellen appears to hold Wonham house in affection since when she and her family leave The Lons they call their residence in Bath, Wonham.[19]

The marriage certificate for Edward and Ellen[20]

The marriage between Edward and Ellen was a very lavish affair. Newspaper accounts describe in detail the packed church, the interior of which was 'adorned with grass, ferns, crotons, lilies, begonias, grass and carnations'. A 160 foot awning was erected 'from the entrance of the churchyard to the door of the church ...adorned with artificial flowers and coloured art muslin.' The townspeople had put up 'triumphal arches' around the town. There was an evening fireworks display and the church bells rang from half past five in the morning until well into the night.[21]

Following their marriage, after a brief spell living in St George, Hanover Square, London, where their first child, Nina Joyce was born,[22] the couple divided their time between residences in Batheaston, Bath and Tiverton before moving into The Lons - Edward had business interests in both areas. It is likely that for a couple of years the family had residences in both places since their second child, Edward Gilbert (1902-1983) was born in Tiverton.[23] Nevertheless Edward resigned as Treasurer to the town council at the end of 1902 stating that he had 'taken up a permanent residence in Bristol'.[24]

The 1901 census shows Ellen living at Southbank, Bannerdown Road, Batheaston with her newly born daughter, Nina Joyce (1900-1984) and four live in servants. Kate Stewart Forbes (1863-1940) is visiting the house. (Interestingly Kate was also a visitor to the Hollond family in Wonham in 1891.)[25] The 1901 census for Tiverton shows Edward to be living at 82, St Peter's Street, Tiverton and although the census states that he is single, this must be an error on the part of the enumerator, who perhaps made this assumption since Edward was the only one living in the house on the date of the census. By 1902 Edward is living at 11, Fore Street, Tiverton and is Borough Treasurer, Council Treasurer and School Board Treasurer.[26] In the same year he is a banker living at South Bank, Batheaston,[27] whilst in 1903 he is appointed to the Board of Guardians for the workhouse in Temple Cloud, Bristol.[28] In 1906 he is listed as joint manager of Stuckey's Bank, 32,

Corn Street, Bristol.[29] These business interests in Bristol and Devon, particularly with regard to Stuckey's bank, continued throughout the time he was living at The Lons.

Inside the Bristol Branch of Stuckeys Banking Co around 1909
Photo courtesy NatWest Group Heritage Hub

The family of four soon became five following the 1909 move to The Lons with Isolde (1910-1992) born there not long afterwards.[30] One can imagine a sumptuous lifestyle for this Edwardian family who enjoyed high society life. The large dining room would have been important for entertaining businessmen and bankers. In 1911[31] the family employed a live-in butler (amongst other servants) so no doubt guests would have been well looked after, whether coming for dinner or staying overnight. It may be that the food was augmented by fruit and vegetables from the gardens and whilst there were cellars for storing quality wines, it may be that the vines from the green houses produced grapes to add to the table's fare. (At a time when cold running water was not generally available, the fact that the green houses are heated by hot water shows just how luxuriously The Lons was fitted out.) Certainly, the family kept the vines and fruit in good condition as Edward advertises for a gardener (single man) to tend the peaches and vineries in 1922.[32]

The friends and business associates who visited The Lons for dinner can only be guessed at from Edward's business and other benevolent interests, but it would appear that they included people of influence. A newspaper account, although dated a couple of years after the family left The Lons, seems to bear this out as it says, *'well known and esteemed of Stuckey's Bank … In business and social circles in Bristol Mr Nicholetts has hosts of friends who read of his son's … with keen satisfaction and congratulation.'*[33] Furthermore, in 1908 when the King and Queen visited Bristol he was invited to attend and be part of the Mayor's party.[34]

As previously stated he worked for Stuckey's Bank and became sole manager of the Bristol branch. Stuckey's was a subsidiary of Parrs Bank and in 1911, Edward also became a Director of Bristol West of England and South Wales Permanent Building Society.[35] He was also a Director of the Bristol Wagon and Carriage Company[36] This latter saw him coming close to court proceedings when shareholders objected to decisions made by the Directors. However the proceedings were stayed, partly because the Directors were *'people well-known and of undoubted solvency in Bristol'.*[37] When Stuckey's Bank was incorporated into Westminster Bank he was the sole manager of the Bristol Branch.[38] It is reported that he took care of his staff and arranged a 'pleasant and informal gathering' when long serving members of staff left the bank.[39]

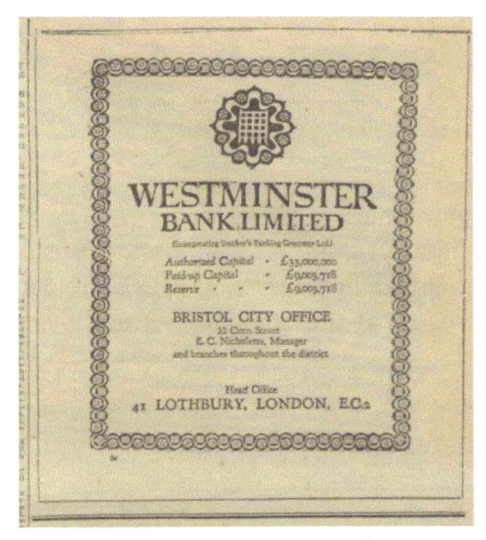

Western Daily Press Jan 25th 1924

Nat West Heritage Companies' website describes how Stuckey's Banking Co Ltd of Taunton, mainly a Bristol and Somerset bank, was taken over by Parr's in 1909 which was itself then amalgamated with London County and Westminster Bank Ltd of London to form London County and Westminster Parr's Bank Ltd. At this point it had 235 branches and 94 sub-branches.

In 1923 the bank shortened its name (unsurprisingly) to Westminster Bank Limited. Eventually in 1970 it merged with National Provincial Bank to become National Westminster Bank.

Edward was a member of The Merchant Venturers and attended their Annual Audit Dinner at Merchant's Hall, Bristol in 1914 – the guest list includes a large number of notable worthies.[40] He was also one of their representatives at the funeral of a Bristol Canon[41]

He supported many charitable causes around Bristol and the local area. For example he became a trustee of the Female Penitentiary known as Magdalen House in Westbury on Trym[42] and was treasurer of The Bristol Royal Blind Asylum or School of Industry for the Blind.[43] He looked to the welfare of animals as well as humans and was vice chair of the subscribers to Bristol Dogs Home[44]. He also supported his wife with her more local charity work.

Edward, at 50 in 1914, was too old to fight as a 3rd Devon Reservist, but he continued his activities with the reservists and supported the war on the home front. He was instrumental in setting up the Bristol Volunteer Regiment[45] and was its joint treasurer.[46] When the war ended he continued with military charity work and was treasurer for donations made in Obligation Week.[47]

OBLIGATION WEEK.

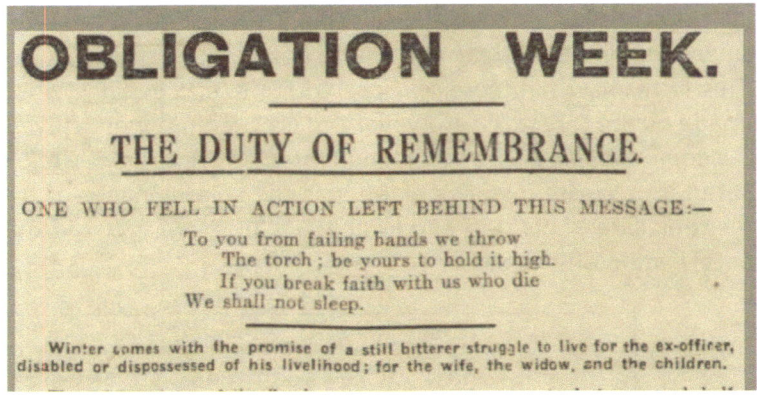

THE DUTY OF REMEMBRANCE.

ONE WHO FELL IN ACTION LEFT BEHIND THIS MESSAGE:—

To you from failing hands we throw
The torch; be yours to hold it high.
If you break faith with us who die
We shall not sleep.

Winter comes with the promise of a still bitterer struggle to live for the ex-officer, disabled or dispossessed of his livelihood; for the wife, the widow, and the children.

Western Daily Press 13th November 1920   *Badge of Bristol Volunteer Regiment[48]*

Edward's work for the war effort involved further social gatherings. For example, in 1919 he attended the Mayor's reception on Durdham Downs, in his role as treasurer for the Bristol Volunteer Regiment, when the war office presented a tank to Bristol in recognition of Bristol's war work.[49] He was also one of 'the distinguished guests'[50] present at the opening of The Moving Pictures Shooting Range in Bristol.

Western Daily Press 25 September 1915

The Bristol Moving Pictures Shooting Range in Baldwin Street was the first to be set up outside London.

A moving picture was projected and at random intervals the image is momentarily frozen. The visitors in the gallery shoot their rifles and there is a light on the screen if the target is hit.

In addition to continuing his membership of the freemasons in the Tiverton Lodge throughout the time he was at The Lons, he was also admitted to The Ancient Order of Foresters at the same time as the Mayor of Bristol and The High Chief Ranger. [51]

So, whilst we do not know exactly who visited the family dining room at The Lons, it is likely that the couple entertained a number of the people Edward met in the course of his public life. With around 'twenty acres of parkland', visitors could use 'the winding drive' to bring their carriages or even motor cars to the front door. No doubt visitors would have been impressed by 'the spacious and lofty entrance hall' with its 'handsome pitch pine staircase'.

When at home Edward may well have used the library for reading and business matters and would probably have kept the key to the strongroom. Nevertheless, Edward was engaged in activities outside of the home for much of the day so it would have been left to Ellen to manage the house, servants and children.

Western Daily Press Wednesday March 4th 1925

Like Edward, Ellen was involved in charity work and local events and may well have held many tea parties similar to the one she held for the NSPCC 'in the drawing room of the Lons'[52] Ellen is the honorary secretary for the Bristol Ladies' Branch of this organisation as well as being the representative for Bitton.[53] There are several newspaper references to her organising whist drives in Oldland and Kingswood for this cause.[54] She directed the ladies in the making of teas for The Longwell Green (Dogs') Home for Waifs and Strays[55] In 1914 she was one of *'the energetic lady helpers'*[56] on the refreshment stall in the marquee at Oldland Fete, held to raise money for a new parish hall. Her daughter, Nina, now aged twelve was helping her. Edward had taken on the role of treasurer for the event. The family wouldn't have travelled far for this as the fete was held on Cryer's field immediately adjacent to Bitton station.[57] The extent of the family's involvement with local church affairs is unclear, although in 1916 the family attended and sent flowers to Canon Henry Nicholson Ellacombe's funeral.[58] In 1924 Ellen and Nina supported Brislington Church Sale of Work. *'Miss Nina Nicholetts of Bitton who performed the opening ceremony was evidently much intrigued by the delightful appearance of the hall.'*[59] Ellen was also supporting the event. Nina enjoyed amateur dramatics and her performance in 'The Lilies of the Field' at Keynsham Drill Hall is praised.[60]

As a fashionable woman of the time Ellen was on the committee of The Bath and Counties Ladies Club and helped organise the ball at The Assembly Rooms, Bath in 1920, her daughter, Nina, also attended.[61] The family enjoyed high society life and there are newspaper reports of Ellen and her daughters attending a number of balls at Bath Pump rooms, supporting the Somerset Light Infantry, Berkeley and Blackmore Vale hunt.[62]

Ellen was an avid golf player throughout the 1920s, winning several competitions.[63] Women's outdoor activities became more popular in the years immediately following the First World War and golf, in particular, became the fashionable sport for wealthy women. Ellen later became secretary of The Lansdown Golf Club when both her daughters had joined her in the sport in 1935.[64] More informal visits from her golfing companions may well have taken place on the veranda outside the dining room or even in the extensive gardens or summerhouse when the weather was good.

Whether the family made use of the three rooms for the Turkish baths is unknown but the baths are still in the house when the property is advertised for sale in 1927.[65]

The family moved to The Lons when Nina was around nine years old and Gilbert seven. The first floor schoolroom would have been used by Nina Joyce and her governess, Olga Oticlie Elizabeth Dluhy (1883-).[66] The governess was from Austria. How long she stayed with the family is not known but in 1922 she left the country to reside in Milwaukee, Wisconsin.

Gilbert may well have had some lessons in the school room but he went to preparatory school shortly after they moved in. His education from age 13 took place at the Royal Naval College, Osborne on the Isle of Wight before going to the Royal Naval College, Dartmouth when he was fifteen years old.[67] This education would have prepared him to be a navy officer although, as we shall see, his illustrious career was with the RAF not the Navy. Certainly from 1913 onwards he would only have been at The Lons for school holidays.

Isolde was born in 1910 so the nurse would have taken care of her in the early years. The nurse was called Susanne Cafferel (1893-) and came from Bobbio-Pellice in Italy. Later Isolde was educated by a governess and intriguingly in 1918 Mrs Nicholetts puts the following advert in a newspaper:

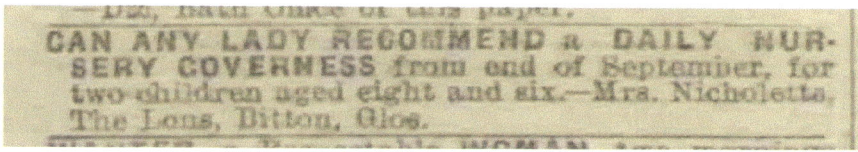

> CAN ANY LADY RECOMMEND a DAILY NURSERY GOVERNESS from end of September, for two children aged eight and six.—Mrs. Nicholetts, The Lons, Ditton, Glos.

Bath Chronicle and Weekly Gazette 20 July 1918

It is surprising that Ellen is looking for a governess for two children. Isolde would be the eight year old but to date the identity of the six year old is a mystery. No birth record has been found for a fourth child in the Nicholetts family and in a number of later records the couple are said to have two daughters and a son. The governess is no longer a live- in governess but a daily one.

With the governess, Olga, born in Silesia, Austria, the butler, Henri Neiniger (1891-) born in Baden Germany only the housemaid Nora Loveder (1892-1976) was local having been born in Bathampton, Bath. (In 1919 Nora married William England,[68] a gardener and lived in Bath until her death.[69] Maybe William was a gardener at The Lons and that is how they met?) Why the family had chosen staff born abroad is not known and little, if anything, has been discovered about their lives after they left The Lons, although Olga moved to America. It is possible that with the start of the war they changed their names. Henri in particular might not have wanted to appear German.

It is unlikely that this family would only have four members of staff. They probably had a number of daily servants - the gardens and outbuildings would definitely have required attention. The house is well set up for staff. On the ground floor is a servants hall, kitchen and back kitchen, pantry, larder, dairy and offices and there are 'principal and secondary staircases' so the servants would have their own staircase. The first floor has six bedrooms and dressing room, providing plenty of accommodation for the family with a bathroom and wc on this floor, the second floor has an attic and lumber room as well as four bedrooms so here there would be ample space for servants and overnight visitors to sleep.

It appears that the family kept a number of staff throughout their time at The Lons as the numerous adverts show. In 1909 Ellen advertises for a parlour maid (single handed),[70] in 1918 for a cook and a parlour maid[71] and in 1920 she was clearly short of staff since she wanted a cook, house parlour maid, under housemaid and between maid.[72] This last advert was in the Exeter and Plymouth Gazette suggesting Ellen may well have found it difficult to obtain servants and was looking further afield. She also advertises in the same newspaper in 1923 for a ' house parlour maid (experienced)- 4 in family; 4 maids kept'[73] The property has a telephone installed by 1925 as in her advert for a cook she gives the phone number as Glos 58218.[74] These are just a few of the numerous adverts placed, many requesting staff to be experienced. Whether servants were in short supply or whether she found it difficult to keep her staff is unknown but in 1920 she is beginning to sound desperate when she places a notice asking, 'Can a lady recommend a parlour maid and housemaid?' She adds that The Lons is situated close to Bitton Station.[75]

Bitton Railway Station Shortly after Closure Photo cc-by-sa/2.0 - © Martin Tester - geograph.org.uk/p/6063329

Entrance Drive to Lons Court Country Estate Willsbridge

Outside the house was no less spectacular and with twenty acres the family would have been able to take long walks and the children had plenty of space for play. It may be that from time to time they took tea in the ornamental summer house. The advert makes no mention of the tennis courts the Sommerville family used but they remain and are referred to in an advert for a gardener in 1922[76] suggesting they were well used by the family during their time at The Lons.

With all of the family's interests in the Bristol and Bath area, transport would have been important. Bitton station is close by but the railway is unlikely to have provided all of the family's transport needs. The Lons had a coach house, stabling, harness room and hay house and whilst to date there is no direct evidence that the family kept their own carriage, horses or later even a car it is likely that a family of this status did so. Certainly Isolde was a keen horse rider and there are several newspaper accounts detailing her riding success so it is likely that she had her own horse.[77]

Life at The Lons was also tinged with sadness for the family, particularly in the early years. In 1908 Edward's uncle, Captain Richard Bremridge Nicholetts (1838-1908) died leaving a wife and daughter who were also very involved with high society life; care needs to be taken not to confuse this family in Clifton with the one living at The Lons. The Captain's funeral was at Bristol Cathedral and is described as 'very impressive'. He had full naval honours with gun carriage covered with the Union Jack and his medals from the Crimean War placed on top. The band from the Clifton Industrial School played the funeral march.[78] Just two years later in 1910 Edward's father died. He had retired to Dawlish on leaving the Weston Super Mare branch of Stuckeys Bank.[79] Edward's mother, Blanche died in 1918 and Edward is one of her executors.[80] In 1912 Ellen's father, John Robert Hollond (1844-1912) died[81] at Stanmore Hall and Edward and Ellen attended the funeral in Stanmore Middlesex. He was buried in the family vault in Stanmore. In 1919 Ellen's mother, Fanny

Eliza Hollond née Keats (1847-1919) also died.[82] She had been living at the Belgrade Mansions Hotel, London and was buried with her husband in the family vault. The family attended the funeral.

So what happened to the family when they left The Lons?

The Lons went up for sale in 1927[83] and whilst this advert is shorter than the 1906 one, its description of the rooms is very similar, so, it would seem that the Nicholetts family, or their landlords, the Alsop children, made very few changes. Nevertheless around ten acres of land had been sold in the meantime reducing its park and gardens by half. (The property was withdrawn at the auction and offered for sale or rent at £160 per annum[84] which gives an idea of the level of rent the Nicholetts were paying.)

It is likely that the family moved to Bath in October 1926 as Ellen advertised for a house parlour maid and housemaid until the end of September for four family members[85] and a cook-general for a maisonette in Bath for the middle of October. In both cases applications are to The Lons. She adds to the latter that there are three in the family and two maids are kept. Gilbert is with the RAF by this time and whilst Nina continues to live with her parents in Brock Street until 1929[86] and at Wonham, Lansdown Road, Bath in 1930,[87] Isolde only returns to live with her parents and sister a couple of years later. It appears that the family continued with their social and charitable commitments when Edward retired to Bath.[88]

Brock Street today (left) and Wonham, Lansdown Road.
Photos from Crisp Cowley website and from Houser on Google website

One of these Brock Street houses would have been the Nicholetts' maisonette. Wonham was where the family settled in Bath. Both houses have recently been sold for several million pounds.

Only a couple of years after moving to Wonham, Ellen died on December 13th 1932[89]. Her funeral took place at St Stephen's Church and she was buried at Lansdown Cemetery.[90]

Nina and Isolde spent time travelling, with Nina visiting Portugal with her cousin Gilbert Poole and his family on at least two occasions.[91] After her marriage Nina and her husband travelled to Sri Lanka and Buenos Aires in 1936[92] and 1938[93]. Isolde travelled to New York in 1938[94]

In 1935 Nina married Harold H. Broadmead, a former High Sheriff of Enmore Castle. The newspaper headline is *'Famous Airman's Sister Weds in Bath'*[95] and a whole paragraph of the account is given over to Gilbert's famous flight. More will be said about Gilbert later. The wedding was lavish and reminds one of Nina's parents' wedding and the high society life the family enjoy. Nina's bridal outfit included the family veil of Chantilly lace and the family pearls. Isolde was one of the bridesmaids. The guest and present lists take up four full columns of newspaper space. The married couple lived in Enmore Castle.[96] Harold died in 1954.[97] Nina left Enmore Castle and died in Taunton in 1984.

Isolde attended a number of lavish weddings, on occasion acting as bridesmaid,[98] and accompanied her father to funerals of people of status.[99] She continued to attend society events. In 1942 she married Christopher J Newman. She died in 1992 in Chichester[100].

Although Edward retired when the family moved to Bath, he continued to contribute to local organisations, for example donating to The Bristol Blind School Swimming Pool Fund in 1950[101]. In 1939, a widower, he remains at Wonham, Lansdown Road but employs a parlour maid, housemaid, cook and nurse. (There is one closed record which from its position could well be another servant, particularly if the nurse is to support Edward who at this point is 76 years old.)[102] Edward appears to have moved to Enmore Castle to live with his daughter and son in law and died there six months after Nina's husband Harold, in 1954.[103]

Enmore Castle, Bridgewater.
Photo from Wikipedia

RAF College Cranwell, Lincs
Photo from Heart of Lincs

Air Marshall Sir Gilbert Edward Nicholetts went on to have an illustrious career following his childhood living at The Lons. Fuller details of his early career can be heard in his interviews for a history project.[104] In this series of interviews he comes across as a modest, private and self-effacing man with a dry sense of humour who is very matter of fact about his achievements. After prep school he, together with some of his friends, had a naval education at Osborne and Dartmouth. This coincided with the end of the war and there was a surplus of naval cadets so he persuaded his parents to allow him to attend the RAF college at Cranwell in 1921 and was one of its first cadets. After a year he was posted to the naval side of aviation and joined HMS Eagle spending most of his time on the ship until 1926 before becoming an inaugural member of the Far East Flight. His first posting kept him from home for over a year with the 'flying boats' and he remained abroad for some time after this. He was awarded the Air Force Cross at this time.[105]

In 1932 he was in a plane crash when, as a flight lieutenant, his flying boat crashed into the Irish Sea. A newspaper report states that he was *'rescued half dead'* with *'cuts to his hands and head'*.[106]

Photo from Bath Chronicle and Weekly Gazette 16 July 1932

Photo from Illustrated London News 20 April 1957

In 1933, together with Squadron Leader Oswald Gayford, he gained a world record for long distance flying, travelling 5,309 miles in 57 and a half hours. The report of the flight was widely celebrated in local and national newspapers throughout the country. In 1958 he received a model of the plane[107] and the fiftieth anniversary of the flight was even celebrated in The Liverpool Echo.[108] Gilbert, himself, says he was 'lucky' to be able to do this as he was a replacement for a Flight Lieutenant who was unwell. On the whole the flying went well, although there was little sleep and the pair lived on black coffee and glucose sweets. A shortage of fuel brought on by strong winds prevented them from flying even further.[109] Gilbert's father and sisters were at the airfield to welcome him home. Nina told journalists how she, her father and sister *'were grouped round the telephone ... anxiously awaiting news and have naturally spent restless nights anxiously waiting for the bell to ring.'*[110] The two airmen were honoured by the King and Gilbert received a bar for his Air Force Cross.[111] In an oral history interview Gilbert makes light of this achievement stating that six months later the record was beaten by a Frenchman.

Gilbert talks of his life with the RAF in the Far East, between the wars, as being very pleasant. He had servants (a batman) who ran his bath, made his tea and kept him comfortable. Social life was in the mess and there was a strict dress code with dinner jackets required some days and mess kits on others. He speaks of it as being *'very disciplined and very comfortable'*. To eat out you needed permission but very few officers had cars for travelling away from the mess. In 1936 he was promoted to squadron leader.[112] In 1938 he worked for the Dept of War Organisation at the Air Ministry where he was responsible for planning air movements throughout the war. However, he said that most of the planning had been completed before the war began. In 1939 he was again promoted, this time to wing commander[113] and lived in the City of Westminster.[114]

Prisoner of War Record for Gilbert Edward Nicholetts   *Coventry Evening Telegraph 4 June 1958*

In 1941 he was again serving in the Far East and when RAF equipment had been left behind by troops who were withdrawing from Sumatra, he took a group of fifty volunteers and ensured that the valuable equipment was rescued. He was mentioned in despatches for this. In March 1942 he was 'missing' and in May 1943 his concerned father puts a notice into the Bath Chronicle and Gazette.[115] Gilbert had, in fact, been taken prisoner of war by the Japanese and remained a prisoner for three and a half years until September 1945.

In 1949 he had his second trip to Buckingham Palace when the King awarded him the insignia of CB (The Honourable order of the Bath)[116] His accolades continued. In 1955 he became an Air Marshall with the position of Air Officer Commanding Malta.[117] In 1956 came another visit to Buckingham Palace but this time to be knighted by the Queen. In the same year he was made an Air Marshall. He was Inspector General of the RAF in 1958-9.[118] In 1959 Air Marshall Sir Gilbert E Nicholetts retired.[119] He died in Wareham, Dorset in 1983.[120]

This portrait below is of Sir Gilbert E Nicholetts is in The National Portrait Gallery.[121]

Sir Gilbert Edward Nicholetts by Walter Stoneman, bromide print, 1954
NPG x186838 © National Portrait Gallery, London

[1] Western Daily Press 11th May 1906 (the property was withdrawn from bidding when it reached £4,750); Western Daily Press 19th May 1906; Bristol Times and Mirror 25th May 1907
[2] Southern and Thornbury Electoral Register
[3] Bath Chronicle and Weekly Gazette 27 April 1927
[4] Southern and Thornbury Electoral Register
[5] Bath and West Weekly Chronicle 26th May 1906
[6] https://www.rafweb.org/Biographies/Nicholetts.htm accessed 20th September 2020
[7] https://www.npg.org.uk/collections/search/person/mp142766/sir-gilbert-edward-nicholetts accessed 23rd September 2020
[8] Baptism record
[9] South Petherton census records
[10] North Devon Journal 24th February 1859
[11] Clifton Society 24th November 1910
[12] 1881 census
[13] Kelly's Directory for 1893
[14] Volunteer Service Gazette and Military Dispatch 16th December 1908
[15] United Grand Lodge of Freemasons, Tiverton register 1893
[16] Westminster Gazette 31 December 1912
[17] https://www.facebook.com/houseandheritage/posts/one-hundred-years-ago-today-wonham-house-at-bampton-in-devon-was-preparing-to-go/2335477046523779/ accessed 26th September 2020
[18] Photos from Facebook and property website https://www.struttandparker.com/properties/wonham accessed 23rd September 2020
[19] Electoral roll Lansdown ward Bath 1930
[20] Photo of certificate courtesy of Ancestry library edition
[21] North Devon Journal 21st September 1899
[22] Birth registration for Nina Joyce Nicholetts
[23] Birth registration for Edward Gilbert Nicholetts
[24] Exeter and Plymouth Gazette 9th December 1902
[25] 1891 Census for Bampton, Devon
[26] Kelly's Directory 1902
[27] Post Office Directory 1902
[28] Wells Journal 15th October 1903
[29] Kelly's Directory 1906
[30] Birth registration for Isolde Nicholetts
[31] 1911 census
[32] Wiltshire Times and Trowbridge Advertiser 16 September 1922
[33] Western Daily Press 10th February 1933
[34] Bristol Times and Mirror 11th July 1908
[35] South Bristol Free Press and Bedminster Knowle and Brislington Record 10th July 1911
[36] Western Daily Press 15th July 1919
[37] Western Daily Press 10th July 1920
[38] Western Daily Press January 25th 1924
[39] Western Daily Press 30th June 1925
[40] Western Daily Press 3rd July 1914

[41] Western Daily Press 17th January 1924
[42] Western Daily Press 27th February 1904
[43] South Bristol Free Press and Bedminster, Knowle and Brislington Record 11th August 1923
[44] Western Daily Press 10th February 1927
[45] Western Daily Press 11th August 1914
[46] Western Daily Press 15th June 1915
[47] Western Daily Press 13th November 1920
[48] http://museums.bristol.gov.uk/narratives.php?irn=11873
[49] Western Daily Press 20th December 1919
[50] Western Daily Press 25th September 1915
[51] Western Daily Press March 4th 1925
[52] Western Daily Press 28th October 1925
[53] Western Daily Press 17th April 1923
[54] Western Daily Press 6th April 1923
[55] Western Daily Press 24th July 1924
[56] Western Daily Press 22nd June 1914
[57] Western Daily Press 22nd June 1914
[58] Western Daily Press 11th February 1916
[59] Western Daily Press 4th December 1924
[60] Western Daily Press 10th April 1926
[61] Bath Chronicle and Weekly Gazette 10th April 1920
[62] Bath Chronicle and Weekly Gazette 11th April 1931; Bath Chronicle and Weekly Gazette 28th April 1928;
[63] Western Daily Press 12th October 1925
[64] Bath Chronicle and Weekly Gazette 18th May 1935
[65] Bath Chronicle and Weekly Gazette 27 April 1927
[66] 1911 Census for The Lons, Bitton
[67] https://www.rafweb.org/Biographies/Nicholetts.htm accessed 26th September 2020
[68] England and Wales Marriage Civil Registration Index
[69] 1939 register and England and Wales National Probate Calendar
[70] Western Gazette 14 May 1909
[71] Western Daily Press 13 August 1918
[72] Exeter and Plymouth Gazette 02 December 1920
[73] Exeter and Plymouth Gazette 07 February 1923
[74] Western Gazette 10 April 1925
[75] Wiltshire Times and Trowbridge Advertiser 09 April 1920
[76] Wiltshire Times and Trowbridge Advertiser 16 September 1922
[77] Western Daily Press 04 August 1925
[78] Clifton Society 03 September 1908
[79] Western Chronicle 02 December 1910
[80] England and Wales Government Probate Death Index
[81] Western Times 01 November 1912
[82] England and Wales Government Probate Death Index
[83] Bath Chronicle and Weekly Gazette 27 April 1927
[84] Western Daily Press 30 April 1927
[85] Bath Chronicle and Weekly Gazette April 1926

[86] Electoral register for Brock Street, Bath
[87] Electoral register for Wonham, Lansdown Road, Bath
[88] England and Wales Government Probate Death Index for Fanny Ellen Nicholetts
[89] Western Daily Press 14 December 1932
[90] Bath Chronicle and Weekly Gazette 17 December 1932
[91] UK and Ireland Outward Passenger lists for Nina Joyce Nicholetts
[92] Passenger list leaving the UK
[93] Passenger list leaving the UK
[94] Passenger list leaving the UK
[95] Bath Chronicle and Weekly Gazette 19th October 1935
[96] 1939 register for Enmore Castle
[97] England and Wales Government Probate Death Index for Harold Hamilton Broadmead
[98] Western Daily Press 12 July 1937
[99] Bath Chronicle and Gazette 27 April 1929
[100] England and Wales Government Probate Death Index for Isolde Newman
[101] Western Daily Press 6 April 1950
[102] 1939 register
[103] England and Wales Government Probate Death Index for Edward Cornewall Nicholetts
[104] https://www.iwm.org.uk/collections/item/object/80003177 accessed 28th September 2020
[105] The Scotsman 01 January 1931
[106] Bath Chronicle and Weekly Gazette 16 July 1932
[107] Coventry Evening Telegraph 13 June 1958
[108] Liverpool Echo 05 February 1953
[109] https://www.iwm.org.uk/collections/item/object/80003177 accessed 28th September 2020
[110] Western Daily Press 09 February 1933
[111] Daily Mirror 12 July 1933
[112] Western Morning News 05 August 1936
[113] Grantham Journal 08 July 1939
[114] 1939 Register
[115] Bath Chronicle and Gazette 05 May 1943
[116] The Western Morning News 02 March 1949
[117] Yorkshire Post and Leeds Intelligencer 29 September 1955
[118] Britain Knights of the Realm and Commonwealth Index from Find My Past
[119] Coventry Evening Telegraph 04 March 1959
[120] England and Wales Government Probate Death Index for Gilbert Edward Nicholetts
[121] https://www.npg.org.uk/collections/search/person/mp142766/sir-gilbert-edward-nicholetts

Chapter 6   Charles Thornton Hall

The Alsop brothers advertised The Lons for sale in 1927[1]. Nevertheless there was no quick sale and it would appear that it was only in January 1929, two years later, that they found a buyer.[2] That buyer was Charles Thornton Hall (1885-1959), an architect and builder.

The advertisement below suggests that the property had not been modernised for some time and that the Alsops and Nicholetts had left it requiring work. The extent of this work can only be surmised. However, modernisation began at once, since within three weeks of the sale a telephone is installed in the name of Charles Thornton Hall. It is interesting to see that a list of telephone subscribers was considered worthy of inclusion in the local newspaper at this time.

Western Daily Press 05 January 1929   Bath Chronicle and Weekly Gazette 26 January 1929

Charles Thornton Hall was well placed to take on the renovations and it is not surprising that he sold The Lons two years later as it may have enabled him to finance his property development business – although this was short lived as the business was in liquidation by the mid nineteen thirties. So what brought Charles and his wife, Gladys to Bitton?

Charles was born in Prendergast, Wales, the son of a baker, Hugh Edward Hall, and his wife Eleanor.[3] He attended school in Pembroke Dock (Upper Meyrick Street) until he was fifteen.[4] By 1901, still in Pembroke Dock, Charles was living with his aunt and uncle, his uncle was a builder.[5] His father was a master baker and two of Charles' older brothers were also bakers.[6] Maybe there was not room in the family business for Charles or he preferred the idea of going into his uncle's building business. Whatever the reason Charles remained with his uncle and aunt and by 1911 was working as an architect and builder,[7] probably for his uncle who employed others. The following year he married Gwladys Mary Breazington (1888-1960), a shoemaker's daughter[8] and music teacher.[9] At some point the family moved to Cardiff where Charles worked as a builder before moving to Weston Super Mare[10] The couple had two children, Morwyth Catherine Hall (1913-1928) and Kenneth D Thornton Hall (1918-).

By 1928 Gwladys, Charles and the children had moved to Hillside Avenue, Kingswood since Charles was involved in 'an important housing contract in Kingswood, Bristol'.[11] Sadly, the couple's only daughter, Morwyth, was killed in a car accident at Cold Ashton crossroads when she was just 15 years old.[12] It would seem unusual to us today that following the accident she was taken by car to her home in Kingswood rather than a hospital. A doctor was called but her injuries were such that she died shortly afterwards.[13]

Morwyth had been the passenger in a car driven by a new driver, Leslie Vernall, a student and family friend. The other driver was the Honourable Diana Darling, daughter of Lord Darling. She did not attend the inquest.[14] Lord Darling was called to give evidence on the driving ability of his daughter even though he wasn't there at the time of the accident! At the inquest Charles also gave evidence and described Vernall's driving as *'very careful'*.[15] Of course this was at a time when a driving test was not required and it was thought by witnesses that he was driving quite fast, around 30 - 45 miles per hour, whilst the other car was travelling at about 12 miles per hour. Details of the accident suggest to the modern reader that the lack of seatbelts in cars at this time may have contributed to her death. This is the account given by the first policeman on the scene as reported in newspaper accounts of the inquest:

P.S.Simmons said that at 3.50pm on Saturday he was on motor-cycle patrol when he came to the scene of the accident. A car was lying wheels uppermost and facing towards Bath, at the Bath and Marshfield corner of Cold Ashton cross-roads.

Further on, the same side of the road, towards Marshfield, he saw another car, which was on the grass, facing towards Bristol with its front near wheel and mudguard against the stone wall. Its interior was devoid of any fittings. On the grass were pieces of broken glass, a wind screen and a seat.

Twenty-seven feet from the rear wheels of the first car, and towards the centre of the cross-roads, he found the start of a wheel skid, and this broadened gradually and finished where the car had overturned. Except for this he found no signs on the road of brakes having been applied. Both cars had been seriously damaged and had to be removed on lorries to Bath.[16]

The inquest reached a verdict of accidental death with errors of judgment on both sides. There is no evidence found to date that anyone was prosecuted for the accident.

The inquest also provides some background on the number of cars on the road in 1928. For example much is made as to whether one of the drivers sounded their horn on approaching the crossroads and there does not seem to be any thought as to who might have had right of way. Clearly this lack of rules can only work with a very small number of cars on the road. The jury's recommendation also provides room for thought as it states that 'the AA be asked to put a scout on the cross roads'.[17]

In 1923 there were 383,525 cars on the road but by 1930 there were one million. By 1938 there were two million. In 2018 there were thirty-five million cars on the road.

Although there were fewer cars in 1928, there were more deaths. In 1926 there were 4,900 fatalities, in 1930 there were 7,305 which compares with 1,900 in 2019.

The Road traffic Act of 1930 was introduced following descriptions of road traffic being 'chaotic'. It introduced third party insurance and abolished 20mph speed limits. Many groups lobbied parliament to abolish all speed limits, not for any safety concerns but because most people ignored them.

In 1932 it was suggested that speedometers in cars become compulsory.

Transport Museum. Road traffic data from various websites[18]

Morwyth died in September 1928 and within six months Charles and Gwladys, together with ten-year-old Kenneth, had moved into The Lons. Did the move have any links to Morwyth's death? Did they want to leave Hillside Avenue because it had too many memories of her? Did they want to remain in the area because Morwyth was buried in Warmley churchyard? Clearly we can only speculate as to their reasons, but whatever they were, the family moved into The Lons in January 1929. The couple continued to grieve for their daughter and a year after her death they inserted the following In Memoriam notice into several newspapers.

> THORNTON-HALL.—In loving memory of our darling Morwyth the only daughter of Charles and Gwladys Thornton-Hall. The "Lons," Bitton, near Bristol, who passed away September 22, 1928. Lovingly remembered by Dad, Mums, and Ken.
> Our hearts just ache with sadness,
> Our eyes shed many a tear;
> God alone knows how we miss her
> As it dawns another year.

Western Daily Press 21 September 1929

Little is known of the two years the family spent at The Lons besides the proposed 'development of the estate'. To date no evidence of what this entailed has been found and it may be that the proposed work was not carried out. Nevertheless it is likely that they kept a car when they were there since in 1934 Charles had been driving one for twenty years.[19]

He was prosecuted for *'leaving a car in a dangerous position'* in 1934. The police constable said that *'the traffic on Terminus Road was brought to a standstill on account of the way in which the car had been left some feet from the kerb'*. Charles said *'he was sorry because it was the first time in twenty years that he had been reported'*.[20] He also explained that he had been unable to get closer to the kerb (the front of the car was five feet away and the back wheels four feet away) due to some bicycles with fruit baskets being parked there. His own solicitor described it as a *'Comedy of Errors'* but nevertheless it was considered worthy of several column inches on two consecutive weeks! He was fined 5s. It is interesting to compare this road traffic offence with the accident which caused Charles' daughter's death. In the latter there is little action taken and none against the drivers of the vehicles in spite of there being *'errors of judgment on both sides.'*[21]

The property was bought by George Lancelot Wood around 1931. Perhaps Charles, having developed the property, was ready to sell at a profit and move on. There is no evidence that he completed any work on The Lons. As yet, it is not known for how much he bought and sold the property so, in view of the poor business acumen he showed later with Kenmore Construction, he may even have sold it at a loss.

Charles and family moved to Eastbourne and then to Harrow where he set up the Kenmore Construction Co Ltd. However things did not go well for him. In 1934 he tendered to build fifty semi-detached houses for £550 a pair but the council felt that they could build the houses themselves at least as cheaply and refused to give him the contract.[22] By 1935 the company was in liquidation and when Charles was sued for £26.5s.8d. for petrol and oil received on credit, he accepted that the goods were received, but says they were for the business for which he was

Managing Director before it went into liquidation. Although his son, Kenneth, also gave evidence that the goods had been for the business, the magistrate ruled that Charles was personally responsible. Charles replied, *'I can make no offer, I put every penny I had in this company and now I am out of work.*[23]

Little is known about the rest of his life. The 1939 register showed him to be living in Bromsgrove, Worcestershire and working as a quantity surveyor for the air ministry. His wife, Gwladys, and son Kenneth were in Newton Abbot. Kenneth became a commercial traveller. He married and moved to Surrey. Charles died in Newton Abbot in 1959[24] and Gwladys in 1960 in Weston Super Mare.[25]

---

[1] Bath Chronicle and Weekly Gazette 27 April 1927
[2] Western Daily Press 05 January 1929
[3] Pembrokeshire baptisms Charles Thornton Hall 20th December 1885
[4] National School Admission Registers and Logbooks
[5] 1901 census for Pembroke Dock
[6] 1901 census for Monkton, Pembrokeshire
[7] 1911 census for Pembroke Dock
[8] Pembrokeshire baptisms Gwladys Mary Breazington
[9] 1911 census for Pembroke Dock
[10] Western Mail 05 October 1928
[11] Western Mail 05 October 1928
[12] Western Daily Press 04 October 1928
[13] Western Daily Press 25 September 1928
[14] Aberdeen Press and Journal 25 September 1928
[15] Bath Chronicle and Weekly Gazette 06 October 1928
[16] Cheltenham Chronicle 29 September 1928
[17] Bath Chronicle and Weekly Gazette 06 October 1928
[18] https://roadswerenotbuiltforcars.com/critical-mass-1923/
https://www.legislation.gov.uk/ukpga/1930/43/pdfs/ukpga_19300043_en.pdf
http://archive.commercialmotor.com/article/19th-february-1929/97/-the-year-1928 all accessed 29 October 2020, road traffic act 1930
[19] Eastbourne Gazette 17th October 1934
[20] Eastbourne Gazette 10 October 1934
[21] Bath Chronicle and Weekly Gazette 06 October 1928
[22] Dover Express 18 May 1934
[23] Eastbourne Gazette 15 May 1935
[24] England and Wales Death Index
[25] England and Wales Death Index

Chapter 7   George Lancelot Wood

George Lancelot Wood (1858-1955) was a successful businessman and a product of Victorian entrepreneurship when around 1931 he moved into The Lons with his second wife, Julia Jane Knill (1861-1937) and his daughter, Ida Gwendoline Wood (1895-1979). He had bought the house from Charles Thornton Hall who, it is believed, had some work done on the estate.[1]

The Lons around the time when the Wood family lived there.

Photo from Find a Grave

Interestingly the house was referred to as The Lawns in this photo, although there are no official documents found to date which give it any name other than The Lons

George Lancelot Wood was the owner and manager of a profitable and well established funeral business which had marketed itself as value for money. It also set out to provide an excellent service for all classes and types of funeral from the time when he set it up in 1879.[2] For Julia, marriage to George was her third marriage: she had previously been the matron of workhouses at Long Ashton[3] and St Albans;[4] a boarding house assistant;[5] and she had worked in an inn.[6] Ida, George's daughter by his first wife, had always lived with her father, carrying out unpaid domestic duties in the home. She did not marry until two months after her father died when she was sixty years old.

So what do we know about George and Julia Wood before they moved into The Lons? At this point they were 71 and 68 years old respectively. Were they looking for a quieter life? Were they ready for retirement? Their lives up until this point may provide some clues as to how they spent their time at The Lons.

George Lancelot Wood's childhood and early life were a good preparation for setting up and running his own funeral business. His father, also called George Wood (1836-aft 1911), was a sculptor living in Clifton when George Lancelot was a baby.[7] Nevertheless, around 1863[8] when George was about five years old, the family moved to College Street in central Bristol and his father, a sculptor and marble mason,[9] took over Henry Cade's marble and stone works, setting up his own business specialising in stone, marble, chimney pieces and other related effects. In fact the Wood family had been trading in marble, stone and statuary since 1700 and previous generations had been working from this College Street site.[10] This background would have provided George Lancelot with the skills he needed to make his undertaker's business successful in providing a full range of services from coffins to marble monuments.

Growing up, George was the eldest of five children (although by 1884 he was the eldest of nineteen children including his step siblings) and his early life was not without difficulties. His mother, Amelia Maria Wall (1835-1871), died at the marble works when he was just thirteen[11] and six years later his widowed father married Louisa née Denman and handed his son, George Lancelot, responsibility for the marble and stone business.[12] Louisa came from a prosperous family of bakers in Bath and she had married a baker. Living and working at the bakery at 3, College Street, a little further up the road from the Wood family,[13] she had been widowed twice.[14] Whether the couple met because they lived in the same street or whether Louisa caught George's eye when arranging the funeral for her husband is unknown. Nevertheless Louisa had been running the bakery after the death of her previous husbands, so it is perhaps not surprising that following the marriage, George Wood Senior moved to the bakery with Louisa, leaving his son, George Lancelot Wood, to run the stone and marble business.[15]

In 1879[16] George married Alice Margaret Wookey (1859-1909) in the Parish Church Clifton and the couple began married life living at the marble and stone works in College Street.

Alice Wookey. Photo taken around 1897 courtesy of Find a Grave

Alice's father, Frederick, had been a publican. He ran The Boar's Head situated in College Place, a little further along the road from the marble and stone works when Alice and George married.

Previously Alice had lived at The King's Head, Back Street, Bristol. Again her father had been the publican there.

By 1881 George had expanded his father's business and was an employer of eight men and three boys. One of his brothers was a marble engraver and one a marble mason.[17] However, not long after this his father decided to return to the marble and stone business. It is perhaps not surprising that a talented sculptor who produced work for the Colston Hall and large memorial tablets for a number of churches (see section on Wood family business) should decide that marble and stone rather than bread was his forte. How George Lancelot reacted when his father returned to the masonry business is unknown, but by 1885 George and Alice had set up their own funeral business at 11, Perry Road.[18] The couple probably responded to an advertisement for 11 Perry Road being for rent. This showed the property included shop, dwelling house and workshops[19] so would have been suitable for both their growing business and growing family. Interestingly the College Street Marble Works incorporated an undertaker's and funeral directors around this time and some of the adverts for the Perry Road business included the phrase 'no connection with any firm of the same name' suggesting that at the very least there was competition between the two businesses.[20]

George Lancelot Wood and Alice had eight children, four boys and four girls,[21] although sadly two of their daughters died young: Alice, aged two, from pneumonia and Gertrude, aged sixteen, from tuberculosis.[22]

The business was profitable and the family were able to engage in leisure activities such as taking a horse drawn wagon on trips into the countryside.

Alice and George's marriage certificate

The Wood family about 1901 including George Lancelot, Alice and children.

Photo from Find a Grave George Frederick Wood

The family continued to live on the premises of the funeral parlour at least until Alice's death in 1909. However, for some reason the probate on her will was not granted until 1926, some seventeen years after she died.[23]

WOOD Alice Margaret of 10 Perry-road St. Michaels **Bristol** (wife of George Lancelot Wood) died 13 February 1909 Administration **Bristol** 31 August to the said George Lancelot Wood undertaker Effects £35 11s. 1d.

Wills and Probate for 1926 from Gov.uk

By 1911 George, aged 52, had moved to The Gables, Gardener Road, Portishead with his daughters Dorothy and Ida, as well as his son Hector, who was still at school. His other sons had remained in Perry Road and were running the business.[24] No doubt he continued to keep an eye on Perry Road since, although he had moved out of central Bristol, he gave his occupation as undertaker and stated that he was an employer on the 1911 census. In June of that year George married the widowed Julia Jane Spencer née Knill (1860-1937).

Julia's life had not been easy. This was her third marriage; she had been through a divorce and the untimely death of her second husband. In 1877 she married John Amer, an innkeeper in Lawrence Hill,[25] but the marriage was not a success and four years later she had returned home to her parents at the Britannia Tavern in Bedminster.[26] In 1894 she instigated an undefended divorce petition against John on the grounds of his adultery and desertion.[27] Divorce was complex and expensive and it is not known how she financed this, but the day after the decree absolute was granted, she married Sidney Spencer.[28] Although a rate collector at the time of the marriage,[29] Sidney soon became workhouse master at Long Ashton[30] before moving to the Hendon union Workhouse in St Albans in 1902[31].

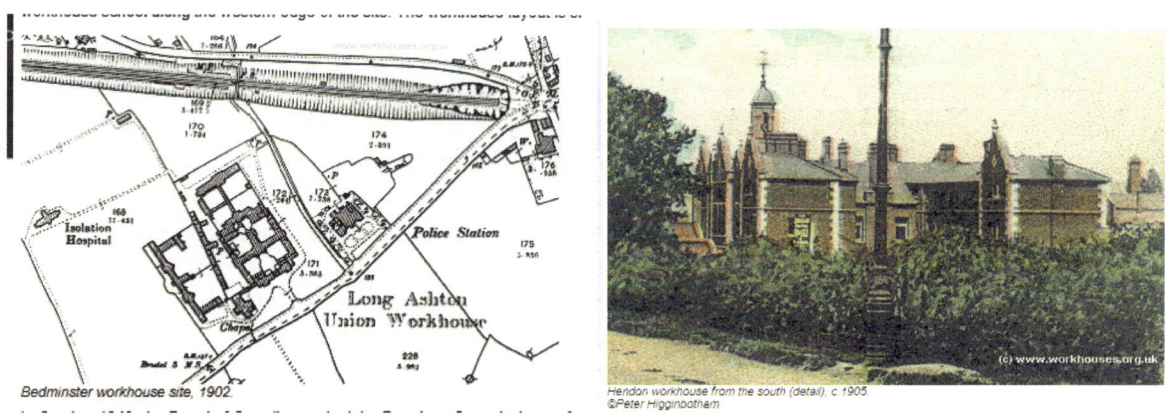

Workhouse layout for Long Ashton and Hendon Workhouse for when Julia and Sidney were Matron and Master[32]

Julia was employed as the matron in both workhouses and the couple appear to have been highly thought of. A newspaper report praised the preparations the couple made for Christmas at the Long Ashton workhouse[33] and when Sidney died in 1908, the local newspaper stated 'both Mr and Mrs Spencer showed great ability in the control and administration of the internal affairs of the Workhouse and their departure was much regretted'.[34] Sidney had suffered from meningitis which affected his brain and the operation to save him was only partially successful. He subsequently suffered from epilepsy and memory loss. Today we would consider the medical treatment of the time to be both unenlightened and unhelpful as Sidney was admitted to hospital in Napsbury (at the time it was known as Napsbury Lunatic Asylum) where he died three years later. The three years of his illness must have been very difficult for Julia and after Sidney's death she returned to Portishead to live with her parents until she married George Lancelot Wood in 1911. The couple lived with George's daughter, Ida, at The Gables in Portishead. The three of them moved to The Lons in 1931.

The family first appeared on the electoral roll at The Lons in 1931 so presumably bought the property from Charles Thornton Hall. What prompted this move is unknown but George continued to run his business in Perry Road from The Lons and gave his occupation as undertaker rather than retired undertaker even when he was 81 years old.[35] No doubt his sons were responsible for the business on a day to day basis.

The family appeared to have kept a low profile when they were living at The Lons. Whilst there are numerous newspaper accounts of village activities during the family's time there, as yet no references have been found to any of the Wood family taking part. Nevertheless George, Julia and Ida can all be found on the electoral roll from 1931 onwards. There were also a number of other people who lived there during their period of residence, most of these were probably staff. The status of Thomas and Minnie Cliff in 1932, Nora Mitchell in 1932 and Grace Mitchell in 1933 and 1934 is unknown. Thomas and Eva Headington were on the electoral roll in 1933 and 1934. Thomas Headington (1879-1970) was the son of a gardener and spent his entire working life in this occupation so presumably he was the Wood family's live-in gardener. He was a widower when he moved to The Lons with his daughter, Eva.[36] When Eva married in 1935 he moved to Cadbury Heath and spent the rest of his life living with one of his daughters in Parkwall.[37]

In 1935 Ruth Ellen Copping was listed on the electoral roll. In 1939 she was working as a nurse companion in Ashley Road, Bristol. It is, therefore likely that she had this role at The Lons. It is possible that Julia was not in good health when Ruth Copping joined the household in 1935. Certainly when George and Ida move from The Lons they advertised a number of items for sale including an invalid folding chair. This may well have belonged to Julia. Julia died on 8th January 1937. George and Ida remained at The Lons and were listed as living there on the 1939 register as well as in Kelly's Directory for that year. The directory also provides some interesting information as to what the area was like at the time.

> BITTON is an extensive parish, in a fertile valley on the London road; it is divided from Somerset on the south by the river Avon, and is 6 miles east-by-south from Bristol, 6 west from Bath and 112 from London, with a station on the Bath extension of the London, Midland and Scottish railway, in the Thornbury division of the county, upper division of the hundred of Langley and Swineshead, rural district of Warmley, petty sessional division of Lawfords Gate, county court district of Bristol, rural deanery of Bitton and archdeaconry and diocese of Bristol. The Boyd brook runs through the village. Electricity is available. Water is supplied by the West Gloucestershire Water Co. The church of St. Mary is an ancient building of stone, in the Norman, Early English and later styles, consisting of chancel, nave, north chantry, and a fine embattled western tower of Perpendicular date, with a stair turret and pinnacles, and containing 8 bells: the north chantry retains three canopied sedilia and a piscina; most of the windows are stained; there are about 700 sittings. The register dates from the year 1571. The living is a vicarage, net yearly value £575, with 12 acres of glebe and residence, in the gift of the Bishop of Bristol, and held since 1916 by the Rev. Frank Henning William Taylor M.A. of St. John's College, Oxford, hon. C.F. There are Methodist and Congregational chapels and Mission halls. There is a Congregational chapel at Oldland Common, and also at Upton Cheyney. In the parish are paper mills and a foundry. The trustees of the late E. A. Whittuck esq. are lords of the manor. The ownership of the land is divided. The soil is loamy; subsoil, rock and coal. The chief crops are wheat and beans, but the bulk of the land is in pasture. The area is 3,665 acres; population in 1931 3,359, and of the ecclesiastical parish, 1,306 (which comprises parts of Bitton and Keynsham, Somerset).
>
> WILLSBRIDGE is partly in this parish and partly in that of Oldland.
>
> BEACH, 2 miles north-east; UPTON CHEYNEY, 1 north-east; and OLDLAND COMMON are hamlets in this parish.
>
> Post, M. O. & T. Office, Bitton. Letters through Bristol
> Post Office, Willsbridge. Letters through Bristol. Oldland Common is the nearest M. O. & T. office
> Post, M. O. & T. Office, Oldland Common. Letters through Bristol
> Police Station, High st. Oldland Common
> Railway Stations (L. M. & S.), Willsbridge & Oldland Common
> Conveyance.—Motor omnibuses from Bristol centre to Bitton & Bath every hour (service augmented on sats.); Bitton to Kingswood (via Oldland Common), hourly, afternoon & evening
> Carriers.—To Bristol & district, Sidney Fry, Warmley, daily; A. G. Adams, North Common, as required

George and Ida remained at The Lons until 1946. In addition to advertising the invalid chair some of the other items for sale were made of marble, no doubt these had been made in the marble and stone works.

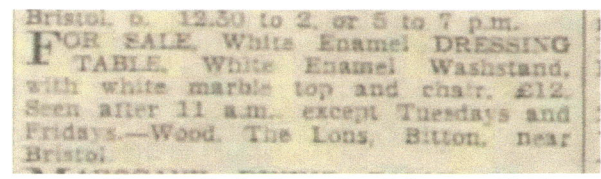

Western Daily Press 1st February 1946   Western Daily Press 5th March 1946

Also in 1946 an E C Winstone appeared on the electoral roll and there was an advert showing him to be selling electrical equipment. Has he moved in after the Woods have left? Was he selling items they had left behind? Or, was he part of the Wood household? There was a Wood family link to electrical equipment since Julia's brother was an electrician[38] and George's youngest son, Harold Hector Wood, became an electrician[39] – the only son not to enter the undertaking business. To date nothing more is known about E C Winstone.

George Lancelot Wood died aged 95 in 1955 and left a reasonable estate of just over £15,500 (worth just over £400,000 in 2020,[40] although his great-grandchildren say that the estate was worth around 12 million US dollars[41]). He had been living in Stoke Bishop at the time. One senses that Ida had spent her life caring for her father and stepmother since she married Robert Francis Walters in Stoke Bishop just two months after her father's death.[42] She died in 1979 aged 75.[43] All the children except Harold, the youngest, were beneficiaries of the will. Harold had refused to take part in the family business and had left home at a young age to be an electrician.[44]

George Wood's Funeral Businesses
G. Wood & Sons and Wood & Co

The undertaker's business, Wood & Co, which George Lancelot Wood ran successfully from Perry Road, Park Row, Bristol whilst living at The Lons, grew out of a family marble and stone works with the business name of G. Wood & Sons. G. Wood & Sons was located in College Street and George had lived on the business premises as a child. He managed it on his father's behalf prior to setting up his own undertaker's in Perry Road. So why did he decide to branch out into undertaking and funerals? Certainly Wood & Co became a very successful business which was continued by George Lancelot Wood's son, George Frederick Wood, and operated until at least 1950 when over 75 newspaper adverts can be found for Wood & Co, Perry Road.

Running a business was not a new venture for the family and it would appear that G. Wood & Sons had been established for many years - since 1700 according to the advert below,[45] although Kelly's Directory for 1880 says, 'established for upwards of a century' and an 1862 newspaper account says 'upwards of 100 years past'.[46] It may well be that the College Street premises had been occupied by the Wood family since the mid eighteenth century but that prior to 1750 the family had conducted the business from another location.

This 1920 advert suggests the business was set up in 1700 so it would have been run by George Lancelot Wood's grandfather and great grandfather. It was also a cemetery contractors. Originally a marble and stone works, George Lancelot Wood may have added the undertakers or maybe his brothers added it when they saw how successful George Lancelot Wood's undertakers had become.

Little is known of the work produced by George Lancelot's grandfather, Henry Wood (1801-1850) but his trade was that of a statuary.[47] It would seem that the family were skilled in masonry, marble work and sculpture from the trades given to them on various census records.

For a few years prior to 1863 Henry Cade (1829-1899) rented the premises in College Street.[48] Whether he had any connection with the Wood family is not known and why he, rather than a Wood family member, was running a marble and stone business on the site after Henry Wood's death[49] has still to be ascertained. Nevertheless Henry Cade came from a family of masons and statuaries.[50] As with the Wood family it would appear that he was very skilled in his trade, producing artefacts as well as practical objects such as wash stands. There is a reference to Cade's architectural masonry in 1860 when he produced a twenty four foot drinking fountain for The Haymarket, Bristol.[51]

George Wood Senior's business, G. Wood and Sons was not a funeral or undertakers but specialised in architectural carving, marble masonry, statuary, sculpting, stone masonry and marble masonry.[52] It was particularly known for its monuments, headstones, tombs and crosses made in marble, stone and granite.[53]

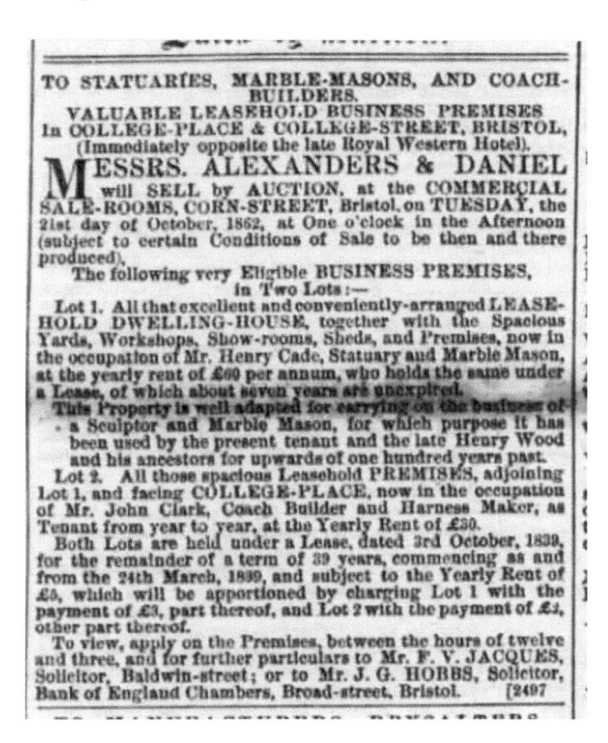

TO STATUARIES, MARBLE-MASONS, AND COACH-BUILDERS.
VALUABLE LEASEHOLD BUSINESS PREMISES
In COLLEGE-PLACE & COLLEGE-STREET, BRISTOL,
(Immediately opposite the late Royal Western Hotel).

MESSRS. ALEXANDERS & DANIEL will SELL by AUCTION, at the COMMERCIAL SALE-ROOMS, CORN-STREET, Bristol, on TUESDAY, the 21st day of October, 1862, at One o'clock in the Afternoon (subject to certain Conditions of Sale to be then and there produced),
The following very Eligible BUSINESS PREMISES,
in Two Lots:—
Lot 1. All that excellent and conveniently-arranged LEASE-HOLD DWELLING-HOUSE, together with the Spacious Yards, Workshops, Show-rooms, Sheds, and Premises, now in the occupation of Mr. Henry Cade, Statuary and Marble Mason, at the yearly rent of £60 per annum, who holds the same under a Lease, of which about seven years are unexpired.
This Property is well adapted for carrying on the business of a Sculptor and Marble Mason, for which purpose it has been used by the present tenant and the late Henry Wood and his ancestors for upwards of one hundred years past.
Lot 2. All those spacious Leasehold PREMISES, adjoining Lot 1, and facing COLLEGE-PLACE, now in the occupation of Mr. John Clark, Coach Builder and Harness Maker, as Tenant from year to year, at the Yearly Rent of £30.
Both Lots are held under a Lease, dated 3rd October, 1839, for the remainder of a term of 39 years, commencing as and from the 24th March, 1839, and subject to the Yearly Rent of £5, which will be apportioned by charging Lot 1 with the payment of £3, part thereof, and Lot 2 with the payment of £4, other part thereof.
To view, apply on the Premises, between the hours of twelve and three, and for further particulars to Mr. F. V. JACQUES, Solicitor, Baldwin-street; or to Mr. J. G. HOBBS, Solicitor, Bank of England Chambers, Broad-street, Bristol. [2497

Advert from Western Counties, Monmouthshire and South Wales Advertiser Saturday October 18th 1862.

The 39 year lease will expire in 1878. However this was renewed since Wood G. & Sons continued to operate there for many years after this.

Whilst it is not known if Henry Cade was in any way related to the Wood family, census records show that he comes from a family of masons and statuaries.

Prior to Henry Cade the property was in the Wood family and Henry Wood, George Lancelot's grandfather and his ancestors had been there for over a hundred years.

In 1863 a number of marble pieces, including chimney pieces and washstand tops were auctioned by Henry Cade in preparation for alterations to the business[54] when the lease was sold to George Wood Senior. He then moved his family and marble business from Clifton back into the shop and accommodation. The advert below provides a good description of the premises when George Wood Senior took over the lease.

George Wood Senior was a talented sculptor of some repute and in 1873 produced two busts for the Colston Hall as well as sculpting tablets in several churches, one being at Saltford Church in 1871. He also constructed a complex monument to an architect's brief for a deceased choirmaster in Arnos Vale Cemetery and it was reported that *'the work has been exceedingly well executed and to the entire satisfaction of the committee.'*[55]

> COLSTON-HALL.—Busts of the late Mr. Robert Charleton and Mr. H. O. Wills have been placed in two of the vacant niches in this hall. These make four busts of Bristol worthies that now adorn the fine building. The two latest are the work of Mr. G. Wood, sculptor, of College-place.

Bristol Mercury 27 September 1873

> Mr. George Wood, of College-place, College-green, was the sculptor of the monumental tablet erected in Saltford church by the Queen Charlton troop of the North Somerset Yeomanry to the memory of the wife of Major Haviland. The work is highly creditable to the sculptor, and gives great satisfaction to the subscribers.

Bristol Times and Mirror 01 March 1871

Many of the funerary pieces he sculpted were very ornate. For example in 1875, following an accident at Teignmouth, Devon where five young people from Bristol were drowned, George Wood Senior produced a lavish sculpture for their grave. The sculpture included a young woman representing the untimely deaths, a picture of a sinking boat on Teignmouth rocks, the names of all those drowned and marble scrolls. This can be seen at Arnos Vale Cemetery.[56]

There are numerous newspaper advertisements for apprentices, stone masons and carpenters for this large and busy company. It would seem that George Wood Senior also encouraged generosity amongst his workforce, since in 1877 his workmen contributed £5.5s.8d. to The Bristol Royal Infirmary. This is only one of several donations reported in the newspapers.[57]

George Wood's Marble Works in College Street

George Wood's Marble Works

The site of George Wood senior's marble and stone works. The business was expanded by George Lancelot Wood before he set up his own business premises in Perry Road, Park Row.

Note the funeral cars as opposed to the horses in the earlier photo.

Date of photo unknown but long after George Lancelot Wood had moved to Perry Road.
Photo from Pinterest

George Wood Senior continued to work well into old age and his census entry for 1911, when he is 75 years old, states that he is the head of his firm and an employer of others, although he may have been a figurehead manager of the company rather than a daily worker at this time. G. Wood & Sons continued long after his death and at least until 1946, although by 1938 the business had moved to 124, St George's Road.

At some point G. Wood and Sons expanded to become an undertakers and complete funeral business – possibly after seeing the success of his son's diversification into funerals. The most likely time for this would have been between 1901 and 1911 when George Lancelot's brothers changed their occupations: Henry Wyndham Wood (1860-1927) from engraver of stone and marble, to monumental sculptor and undertaker;[58] Arthur Wake Wood (1862-1934) supplemented his income by working as a tobacconist as well as a sculptor.[59] At this time Arthur moved to Woolwich, London to be foreman of a marble works,[60] again suggesting that the business needed to diversify. This expansion into undertaking would have been a natural progression since many of the marble and stone ornaments and artefacts were linked to the lavish funerals which wealthy Victorians favoured. The family would have realised that their premises required few alterations to make coffins and other funeral effects. Adding transport provided further opportunities to offer a complete funeral service.

It was into the marble and stone business that George Lancelot Wood was brought up. In 1879 he took over the business[61] and by 1881 he employed eight men and three boys whilst working as a marble mason.[62] He continued to live at the marble works whist his father was running a bakery (together with his second wife) further down the road. His brothers, Henry and Arthur were living and working with him.[63] However, by 1883 George Lancelot had left his father's business and set up his own funeral and undertakers, first at 5, Perry Road[64] and then at 11, Perry Road[65].

However, one wonders if there was some rivalry between George Lancelot Wood and his brothers since Perry Road adverts increasingly state that Perry Road is the only address for the business and others state there is no connection with other funeral businesses of similar name. Wood and Co. and Wood G. and Sons were clearly two very separate businesses.

By 1884 George's Perry Road business has expanded and he was running a complete funeral service.[66] This would have made good entrepreneurial sense since Victorian funerals for the wealthy were lavish affairs and he was already making the sculptures and monuments which accompanied them. Even the poorer sections of society would save for their funerals through insurance schemes and there are accounts of families going without food to ensure they had enough money to bury an infant should it die. Mortality rates were still high at this time.[67] However, no doubt the real money lay in the extravagant funerals with a hearse and several mourning carriages together with a luxurious coffin with polished brass adornments – all of which George Lancelot Wood was keen to provide. It is quite possible that George Lancelot saw diversification as the best way forward for his business. Although he was a skilled mason, towards the end of the nineteenth century demand for the very ornate tomb decorations was beginning to wane and he would be able to continue to produce these when they were required for the wealthy, but he could also provide a service for many more people with a funeral business which catered for all. The marble and stone monuments would have been ordered by a funeral furnisher so by extending the business to include coffin making and undertaking he would have been able to extend his business offering and maximise his profit.

It is clear from the many newspaper adverts from 1884 onwards that George's marketing strategy was low prices, value for money and funerals arranged for all classes of people.

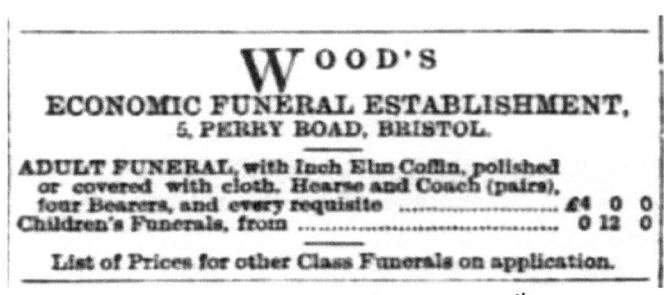

WOOD'S ECONOMIC FUNERAL ESTABLISHMENT, 5, PERRY ROAD, BRISTOL. ADULT FUNERAL, with Inch Elm Coffin, polished or covered with cloth. Hearse and Coach (pairs), four Bearers, and every requisite .... £4 0 0 Children's Funerals, from .... 0 12 0 List of Prices for other Class Funerals on application.	REFORM FUNERAL FURNISHERS. WOOD & CO., Complete Undertakers & Funeral Directors, 11, PERRY ROAD, ST. MICHAEL'S, BRISTOL. FUNERALS COMPLETELY FURNISHED in a Superior Style with Every Requisite, including all Fees and Expenses, according to a Fixed Scale of Charges, regulated to suit all Customers, and with a strict regard to economy in every detail. ESTIMATES GIVEN FOR FUNERALS TO ANY EXTENT.
Western Daily Press, Bristol, August 13th 1884	*Clifton Society July 7th 1892*

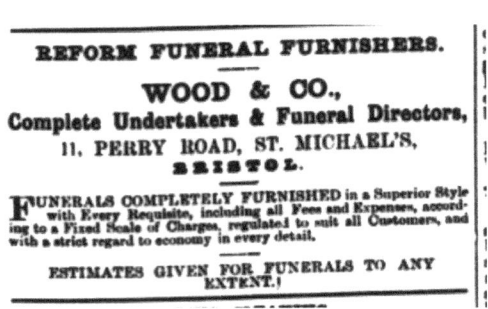

The advert from 1884 is shortly after he moved to Perry Road and there is a sharp focus on economy. The second advert shows him to be a reform funeral furnisher. It is interesting to see how his description has changed from that of a 'funeral establishment' to being a 'funeral furnisher'. Traditionally funeral furnishers were considered to be superior to undertakers and coffin makers. On being asked to arrange a funeral they would first assess the wealth of the family of the deceased in order to suggest arrangements appropriate to the class and wealth of the deceased. They would then arrange for the body to be washed and measured for a coffin, this could be very sumptuous with expensive coffin furniture for the wealthy. The funeral furnisher would also outsource the transport requirements, arrange for tombstones and monuments to be made and pay all the tradesmen as well as the burial fees – obviously these would be reclaimed as part of the final bill.[68] However it is clear from the situations vacant adverts in newspapers that George Lancelot Wood provided most, if not all, of the services with his own workforce which would have increased efficiency and also profit. It would appear that he was keen to ensure that he could employ workers living a distance away since in 1883 he was part of a pressure group to support the extension of the London and South West Railway to Bristol. The aim was to stop a GWR monopoly and allow workers from the countryside to access employment in Bristol.[69]

A Victorian Funeral and the area of Perry Road where Wood & Co operated[70]

By 1893 George Lancelot's business was well established. He has an entry in the directory for the Ports of Bristol Channel which mentions its *'moderate charges'* and meeting *'the requirements of all classes'*[71]. It states that *'the management of the firm must certainly be assigned the highest praise'*.

> **Wood & Co., Complete Undertakers,** Perry Road, Bristol.—The above-named business was originally established in 1879, by the present sole representative of the firm, Mr. G. L. Wood, who has since continued the concern with steadily progressive success, trading under the style of Messrs. Wood & Co. The premises occupied by the firm are situated at 10 and 11, Perry Road, and comprise a commodious establishment, replete with every convenience and requisite for the efficient carrying out of a business of this character. The firm undertakes the complete furnishing and conducting of funerals of every class, providing all the necessary accessories and equipment, and performing all the duties attached to these last solemn rites with befitting decorum. A staff of able and intelligent assistants is employed to carry out the arrangements, and in the completeness and efficiency of every detail of the management the firm must certainly be assigned the highest praise. We may also add that the trade is supplied with every requisite. The business is carried out under the immediate personal supervision of the principal, whose courteous and unremitting attention to the requirements of all classes, combined with high-class style at moderate charges, have established for Messrs. Wood the well-won position the firm deservedly enjoys.

From Progress Commerce 1893: Ports of the Bristol Channel; Wales and the West

As can be seen from the adverts below, the approach of providing all the services linked to a funeral, together with value for money did not change. By 1902 he has added embalming to the services he offered as well as undertaking cremations.

G. L. WOOD, UNDERTAKER,
THE BEST AND CHEAPEST FUNERAL FURNISHER,
Perry Road (bottom of St. Michael's Hill, Bristol. 1047

Bristol Daily Post, May 11th 1888

WOOD & Co., Undertakers and Funeral Carriage Proprietors, 10, Perry Road, Park Row, Bristol. Funerals at Lowest Charges. Personal Attendance. Distance no object. Tel. 1249.

Western Daily Press 8th November 1910

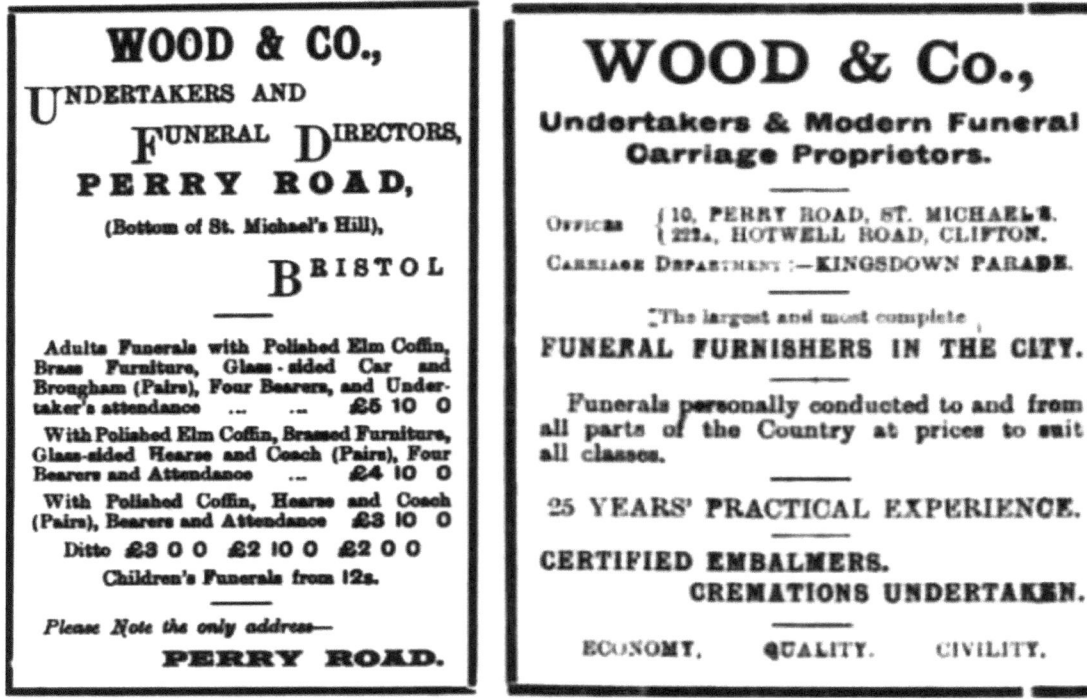

WOOD & CO.,
UNDERTAKERS AND
FUNERAL DIRECTORS,
PERRY ROAD,
(Bottom of St. Michael's Hill),
BRISTOL

Adults Funerals with Polished Elm Coffin, Brass Furniture, Glass-sided Car and Brougham (Pairs), Four Bearers, and Undertaker's attendance ... £5 10 0
With Polished Elm Coffin, Brassed Furniture, Glass-sided Hearse and Coach (Pairs), Four Bearers and Attendance ... £4 10 0
With Polished Coffin, Hearse and Coach (Pairs), Bearers and Attendance £3 10 0
Ditto £3 0 0 £2 10 0 £2 0 0
Children's Funerals from 12s.

Please Note the only address—
PERRY ROAD.

WOOD & Co.,
Undertakers & Modern Funeral Carriage Proprietors.

OFFICES: 10, PERRY ROAD, ST. MICHAEL'S.
222a, HOTWELL ROAD, CLIFTON.
CARRIAGE DEPARTMENT:—KINGSDOWN PARADE.

The largest and most complete
FUNERAL FURNISHERS IN THE CITY.

Funerals personally conducted to and from all parts of the Country at prices to suit all classes.

25 YEARS' PRACTICAL EXPERIENCE.

CERTIFIED EMBALMERS.
CREMATIONS UNDERTAKEN.

ECONOMY.   QUALITY.   CIVILITY.

The Horfield and Bishopston Record and Montpelier Free Press
November 20th 1897 and January 11th 1902

Newspaper funeral notices also bear out the wide range of funerals which the company arranged, from a member of the National Opera Company who died when touring in Bristol in 1922 and required a Roman Catholic funeral, to a multi-carriage funeral attended by 'a large gathering of anglers at Greenbank Cemetery' in 1904 and many others at Arnos Vale including two on the same day in 1937, an antiques dealer and a solicitor.[72] Certainly from at least 1916 onwards the firm was offering a choice of 'motor hearse or funeral carriage' and would conduct funerals in town or country. The business was also on the telephone at this time.[73] It continued to keep up with changes in funeral practices and by 1937 mentions Daimlers as opposed to motor vehicles in its adverts.[74] In 1946 Wood & Co was advertising in the telephone directory with a large advertisement. This single phone book covered a very wide area showing how few people had their own telephone but this eye catching advert at the bottom of the page would be easily seen by people looking for a Bristol undertaker.

'Phone: BRISTOL 22949

WOOD & CO. (Undertakers) LTD.

FUNERAL & CREMATION DIRECTORS
MOTOR HEARSE AND FUNERAL CARRIAGE PROPRIETORS

PLEASE NOTE THE ADDRESS **10, Perry Road, Park Row, Bristol. 1**

British Phone Books 1946 for Portsmouth/ Southampton/ Bournemouth/ Exeter/ Plymouth/ Taunton/ Bristol/ Gloucester South

Of George's four sons, three followed him into the family business, George Frederick Wood (1879-1962), Percy Wyndham Wood (1881-1963) and Frederick Lancelot Wood (1891-1962). Harold Hector Wood (1898-1973) became an electrical engineer.

George Frederick and his family lived in Kingsdown Parade, the site of the second undertakers belonging to George Lancelot and the third establishment in Bristol which bore the Wood name. By 1939 he is living in Southwell Street, Kingsdown[75], and a short distance from the undertaking business. He was one of the coffin makers and continued to work until the age of 80 only retiring in 1959.[76]

Percy continued to live at Perry Road for a few years after he married before moving to Portishead where his wife set up a confectionery shop and ran a cafe.[77] Percy continued to work in his father's undertaking business except for a short time during the war when he was in the RAF.[78]

Frederick Lancelot and his sister Dorothy continued to live on the premises in Perry Road. He was joined by his wife in 1947 when he married[79] and remained there until his death.[80]

The business was still operating in 1958 as there is a death notice for that year stating that 'flowers to go to Wood and Co undertakers, Perry Road, Bristol'. It is likely that it closed in 1959 when George Frederick retired.

---

[1] Western Daily Press 05 January 1929

[2] Progress Commerce 1893: Ports of the Bristol Channel; Wales and the West. Accessed from Bristol Industrial Archaeological Society (BIAS) on 7th September 2020
https://www.b-i-a-s.org.uk/images/pbc040.jpg

[3] 1901 census

[4] Hendon and Finchley Times 01 May 1908

[5] 1911 census

[6] Marriage certificate for the parish church in the parish of Holy Trinity, Bristol

[7] 1861 census and baptism record for George

[8] Bristol Daily Post 05 August 1853
[9] 1871 census
[10] Western Counties, Monmouthshire and South Wales Advertiser October 18th 1862
[11] Western Daily Press 28 October 1871
[12] England and Wales Marriages 18 September 1877 – Louisa Davie and George Wood
[13] 1871 Census for College Street Bristol
[14] Louisa married Henry Lucas on 10 April 1860 and he died April 1864. She married George Davie in February 1871 and he died in 1876.
[15] Kelly's Directory 1879, 1880 and 1881 census
[16] England and Wales Marriages 19 January 1879 – George Lancelot Wood and Alice Wookey
[17] 1881 census
[18] Western Daily Press 05 September 1885
[19] Western Daily Press 26 May 1884
[20] Western Daily Press 04 March 1913
[21] George Frederick Wood (1879-1962); Percy Wyndham Wood (1881-1963); Dorothy Gladys Wood (1893-1986); Frederick Lancelot Wood (1891-1962); Ida Gwendoline Wood (1895-aft1955); Harold Hector Wood (1898-1973); Gertrude Maud Wood (1888-1904); Alice Amelia Hannah Wood (1885-1887)
[22] https://www.findagrave.com/memorial/47558024/george-frederick-wood accessed 18th October 2020
[23] England and Wales National Probate Calendar 1926 Alice Margaret Wood
[24] 1911 census
[25] England Select Marriages, Holy Trinity, Bristol John Amer and Julia Jane Knill.
[26] 1881 census for Bedminster
[27] England and Wales Civil Divorce Records 1858-1918 Julia Jane Amer and John Amer
[28] Bristol Church of England Marriages and Banns Julia Jane Knill and Sydney Spencer
[29] Bristol Select Church of England Parish Registers Easton, St Gabriel, Gloucestershire, Julia Jane Knill and Sidney Spencer
[30] 1901 Census Long Ashton
[31] Hendon and Finchley Times 01 May 1908
[32] http://www.workhouses.org.uk/Bedminster/ and http://www.workhouses.org.uk/Hendon/
[33] Bristol Times and Mirror 26 December 1901
[34] Hendon and Finchley Times 01 May 1908
[35] 1939 register
[36] Parish record for St Barnabus Church, Warmley. Marriage of Eva Millicent Headington
[37] Electoral roll for Cadbury Heath
[38] England and Wales probate for Julia Wood
[39] Harold Hector Wood attestation papers 1916
[40] CPI inflation calculator
[41] https://www.findagrave.com/memorial/47558024/george-frederick-wood accessed 18th October 2020
[42] England and Wales Marriages Ida Gwendoline Wood and Robert Francis Walters 7th April 1955
[43] England and Wales Civil Registration Death Index
[44] https://www.findagrave.com/memorial/47558024/george-frederick-wood accessed 18th October 2020
[45] Horfield and Bishopston Record and Montpelier and District Free Press 04 June 1920
[46] Western Counties, Monmouthshire and West Wales Advertiser 18 October 1862
[47] 1841 census
[48] Kelly's Directory 1856

[49] Western Counties, Monmouthshire and West Wales Advertiser 18 October 1862
[50] 1841 census
[51] Western Daily Press 31 March 1860
[52] https://sculpture.gla.ac.uk/view/organization.php?id=msib1_1220430742&search=stone accessed 30 October 2020
[53] J Wright and Co's Bristol and Clifton Directory 91st edition 1889
[54] Bristol Daily Post 05 August 1863
[55] Bristol Mercury 21st March 1879
[56] Western Daily Press 12 June 1875
[57] Western Daily Press 24 February 1877
[58] 1901 and 1911 census records for Henry Wyndham Wood
[59] 1891 census for Arthur W Wood
[60] 1901 census
[61] Kelly's Directory 1879 and 1880
[62] 1881 Census
[63] 1881 census
[64] Western Daily Press 23 January 1883
[65] Western Daily Press 11 December 1888
[66] Western Daily Press Bristol 13 August 1884
[67] The Victorian Celebration of Death by James Stevens Curl
[68] https://regencyredingote.wordpress.com/2012/10/19/the-regency-way-of-death-furnishing-the-funeral
[69] Western Daily Press 23rd January 1883
[70] Photos courtesy of Flickr.com and Google maps
[71] From Progress Commerce 1893: Ports of the Bristol Channel; Wales and the West. Accessed from Bristol Industrial Archaeological Society (BIAS)
[72] Western Daily Press 22nd February 1937
[73] Western Daily Press 2nd May 1916
[74] The Western Daily Press and Bristol Mirror December 2nd 1937
[75] 1939 register for George Frederick Wood
[76] https://www.findagrave.com/memorial/47558024/george-frederick-wood accessed 30 October 2020
[77] 1939 register
[78] RAF service record
[79] Marriage index for Frederick Lancelot Wood and Gladys Julia Victoria Cox
[80] Probate record for Frederick Lancelot Wood

Chapter 8   Norman Hall and Eezall

Norman Abbott Hall and Alexandra (Queenie) Hall were the residents of the Lons for just a short period from 1948 to 1952. They were an extraordinarily rich family, as a result of building up a business in washing powder inherited from his father.

Herbert Hall
At the time that Norman and Alexandra were married in 1924 he was 27, a Works Manager for his father's firm, and she was 21, daughter of a Commercial Traveller. Norman's father Herbert had started a soap powder business, H.E. Hall Manufacturing Co., trading under the name 'Eezall' from a house in Stapleton – Estcourt House in Park Road and then at Downend Road in Kingswood.

His father seems to have been a colourful figure. He was actively associated with Stapleton Parish Church where he was a church warden at the time of his death. In 1901 he was a Commission Agent (a salesman employed on a commission-only basis). He was at one time chairman of Stapleton Ward Conservative Association. In discussing him at his funeral the rector said that 'He was a remarkable man and one only had to be with him for a short time to realise his great qualities. He was so dauntless…He had a disdain for undue caution.' This was born out by the fact that he was successfully prosecuted in 1902 for running bets as a bookmaker in a public house, the Russell Arms in Lawrence Hill.[1] At the time of his death in 1933, at age 62, he left a comparatively small estate, compared with the size the business was to become, - £3,000 (£200,000 in today's value).[2]

Estcourt House, Park Road, Stapleton in 2020

Norman Hall's continuation of his father's business
After his father's death, Norman expanded the business with factories in Oldland Common (at the bottom of the 'Turnpike' Barry Road), in Hanham (at John Wesley Road), with offices and a yard at Willsbridge. Keith Short remembers that he earlier operated from 'Querns' a large stone-built house opposite the garage in Willsbridge, where local people worked filling boxes with his washing powder.[3] He later built Berry House, Wick, where he again produced his washing powder products.[4]

Shire Horses

Norman, like his father, used Shire horses for his delivery wagons. His teams of magnificent Shire horses were a feature of the district for many years. He also had a farm in Caerleon, which he used to visit at weekends. This was in part just a hobby, but he used the farm as a nursery and rest centre for his Shire horses. He was very fond of horses and at one time had as many as 20 Hunters in his stables, using them to ride with the Llangibby Hunt in Monmouthshire. Norman owned about 10 or 12 horses which were

Date unknown: photo courtesy Paul Townsend

kept at Willsbridge, some Shire and some show jumping horses. Bert Legge was his jockey, and he was helped in the stables by his brother, and Wally Hemmings, a local man who lived in Cherry Gardens, who, was also a foreman in the factory.[5] It was an impressive sight to see the string of horses, saddled up and walking up the road. They were put out to graze on what is now Fonthill Garden Centre.[6] He was a Freemason, a keen churchman and was for some time a churchwarden at Oldland Parish Church where he also ran a young men's club.[7]

Chewton Place

Norman and Alexandra moved to The Lons in 1948. They previously lived at High Street Oldland Common from 1927 to 1934 and then moved to Chewton Place, Keynsham in 1934. Chewton Place House was a similar sprawling mansion to the Lons and now a conference centre. It is Grade 11 listed and built circa 1762. Chewton Place has 18th-century pleasure grounds, bounded by the river Chew, and a ha-ha. It contains a rubble-built folly tower, known as the Owl Hoot.[8]

In the 1939 Register before the start of World War II their address is shown as 258 Bath Road Keynsham. This may have been a temporary residence before they moved to the Lons.

For the first half of the twentieth century Chewton Place was occupied by a series of

Chewton Hall, Chewton Place

76

tenants and its condition fluctuated with their means and lifestyle. In 1934 Mr & Mrs Hall moved in. They were enthusiastic amateur musicians and arranged concerts, garden parties and light opera performances in the garden. Chewton Place was a popular venue, its huge trees and banks of shrubs making a perfect backdrop for the performers. In about 1928 school pupils gave a performance of the Pied Piper of Hamlin. Others remember a splendid performance of a Midsummer Night's Dream. In 1934 an ambitious event was planned in aid of Chewton Scouts. After a Garden Party, opened by Lady Helena Gibbs, a niece of Queen Mary, a performance of the operetta San Marino, with full orchestra, was to be given by the Oldland Amateur Operatic Society. Armchairs on the terrace cost 2/6d and deck chairs on the lawn 1/-. After a boiling hot day the performance began splendidly, but immediately after Act 1 there was a tremendous thunderstorm: the heavens opened, the singers, orchestra and audience fled to the house for shelter where the occupants, Mr and Mrs Hall, lit fires to dry them out. The rest of the performance was abandoned.[9]

They moved to Beckington in Somerset in 1961 which is where they lived at the time of his death in 1974.[10]

Norman had a very expensive car which would have turned heads, not just because there were few cars in the late 1940s, but because it was such an expensive model – a Daimler 36 limousine, colour maroon. It was bought in 1947, originally specified by the Maharaja of Baroda but not delivered to the Maharaja. It was purchased for £4,700 (£185,000 at 2020's value).[11]

As an employer, Mr Hall was known for his generosity and helpfulness to any employees and other acquaintances when they were in need of aid. The large gathering at the funeral included a

1947 Daimler DE 36 Limousine Landaulet: photo source Wikiwand

number of former employees and other old friends. Keith Short remembers going there on a Saturday morning, with his friends to help load the boxes on to a horse drawn trailer for half a crown each (2 shillings and 6 pence) which is worth £7.50 today. Also, at Christmas, they would go carol singing there, and were invited in the house, and again, were given a half a crown each.[12]

Norman served in France In the First World War. He was gassed and suffered severely from rheumatism, being in hospital for a year. In the Second World Was he was an air raid warden at Bitton. The Halls had three children and eight grandchildren. The son, John Hall, MA, became a playwright and broadcast writer and headed the Open University of Scotland. A number of his plays have been staged at the Bristol Theatre Royal. [13]

Eezall

Many say that *Eezall* was not much help with the wash. However, anything which made a slight improvement when washing by hand and made the water softer must have been welcomed.

Eezall was described as gold medal oxygen washing compound. It was awarded gold medals and diplomas at shows in Bournemouth, Portsmouth, London, Harrogate, and Wembley. They claimed that it saves hours at the wash tub. In the 1940s it was advertised as a product that was first introduced nearly 40 years ago and that Granny had used Eezall years and years ago. Also, that there is nothing like it for the big family wash, for dirty overalls, etc., and for washing up after meals, with no scum or grease. Eezall was made from sodium carbonate (washing soda) and sodium silicate.

In the mid 1930s detergents based on phosphates became available first with *Dreft* (which was later re-launched for delicate fabrics and baby clothes). These worked by breaking up oils and grease to float away the dirt but left the clothes hard and stiff. N.A. Hall Manufacturing had a reprieve from development of better synthetic detergents by Proctor and Gamble because World War II led to shortages of some of the raw materials used in the new formula detergents.

Miss Eezall

Our washing day was once so long,
Without a smile, without a song,
What did I need to change the wrong?
Miss Eezall
Who saved my elbows from the tub?
Who taught my knuckles not to rub?
And made the oilcloth need no scrup?
Miss Eezall
What do I care if dress be soiled?
And blankets, sheets and suts look 'moiled'?
Who saved me from a life near spoiled?
Miss Eezall
Who made the washing seem a joke?
While I can sew and Jack can smoke?
(The dirties only need to soak)
Miss Eezall
Who is it cleans by day or night?
Who makes our garments snowy white?
Who sends the microbes off in fright?
Miss Eezall
Who when 'spring cleaning' comes our way?
Gets one week's work done in a day,
While we just Fourpence only pay?
Miss Eezall
Who keeps our hands so soft and white?
And makes our ornaments so bright,
Our glass and curtains a delight
Miss Eezall
From her I never will depart!
I sing her praise – she won my heart!!
With her YOU'D better make a start!!!
Miss Eeezall

Western Daily Press, February 5, 1944

78

By the late 1940s Proctor and Gamble introduced *Tide*, and Crosfields' of Warrington (a subsidiary of Lever Brothers) introduced *Surf*, products which would have a dramatic effect on sales of *Eezall* and other soap-based products (even if it was 'what Granny uses').

At that time a typical way of selling soap was to have a demonstration and to offer sample packets for trial at home. It would take us another fifty years to find that these newer phosphorus-based agents, although generally non-toxic, caused nutrient pollution with serious environmental consequences.[14]

N.A. Hall's competitors Lever Brothers, which became part of Unilever has a sorry history, notably coming under criticism for the use of forced labour in Africa.[15]

Michael Lear remembers that Persil offered to buy out N.A. Hall Manufacturing but that Norman Hall declined, which he probably later regretted as Eezall sales declined in favour of popular brands based on newer formulations.[16]

Doing the laundry before washing machines and detergents was as an arduous, seemingly endless task. For most families it was a weekly task that started on Monday. Clothes were often badly soiled from physical work, with the 'Sunday best', required for church. On a Sunday evening, copper and dolly tubs might be filled with cold water in preparation for wash day on Monday. Clothes were sorted and segregated into woollens and cottons and colours and whites. Dirty clothing like overalls would be left to soak overnight with soap flakes added. White shirts and blouses would stand overnight in cold water containing a "blue" whitener. At the start of wash day the electric copper was turned on, or a coal fire was lit under the brick copper to ensure that the water in the tubs was hot enough (in Upton Cheyney, which was not supplied with running water until 1962, the task was doubly difficult). A

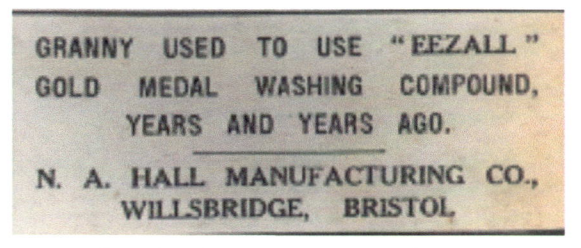

Advertisement; Western Daily Press, 4th September 1943

dolly peg would be used to agitate the items that had been soaking overnight. On wash day, most rooms in the home were dull, steamy, and damp. After the steam had cleared, the next part of the process was the ironing. The washing process itself involved lifting the items from the cold soak and wringing or mangling each item before transferring them, with more soap flakes, into the copper for boiling. Items that remained soiled, even after an overnight soak, were rubbed on a scrubbing board before being transferred to the copper.

A clothes mangle, a hand operated machine consisting of two rotating rollers (mind your fingers!), would be used to squeeze out all the excess water. Hopefully it wasn't raining, and clothes could be hung out to dry on a clothes line, otherwise they had to be laid over a clothes-horse next to the kitchen or living room fire. Often by the time the washing, drying and ironing tasks had been fully completed, wash day had come back around again![17] Anything which made that task easier or helped to make the clothes look cleaner was worth spending money on and hence Eezall became big business.

As well as Eezall washing powder, the company also branched into lavatory cleaning products with 'Lavdust'. In the 1930s they also produced 'ALFA' oxygen washing tablets, 'I X L' laundry compound, and 'KLEENALL' cleaning powder for dairies, butchers, bakers, ice cream venders etc. It is not known how successful these products became.

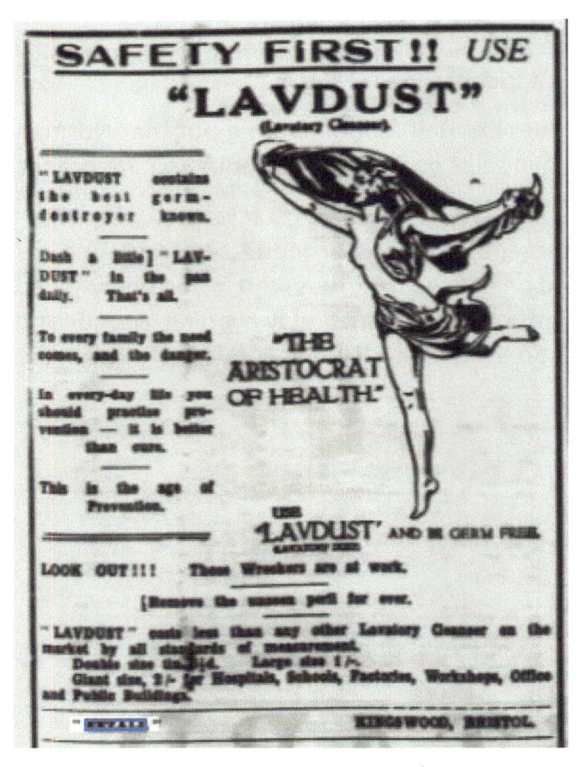

Advertisement, Western Daily Press, 5th August 1943

The company of N. A. Hall Manufacturing Co. (Willsbridge), Ltd., was wound up by voluntary liquidation, in July 1953, no doubt due to the launch of the technically superior phosphorus-based products such as *Tide*. The assets of the company were put on sale by auction in August 1953 after being in business for 40 years.[18] Included for offer at the sale was the large saloon Daimler car, bought by Mr. N. A. Hall in 1947. Among other lots being sold were thousands of paper bags, about 40,000 small bottles, numerous cardboard cartoons and four tons of crushed soda crystals. There were also large quantities of the articles used as gifts in promoting the product, such as toothbrushes, silk stockings, and nightdresses. In the mechanical line there were hand-operated jib mobile cranes, air compressors, electric drills and spanners. Typewriters, desks, filing cabinets, chairs were part of the office equipment.

Within an hour and a half of the sale 284 lots were sold. The highest bid was £5 15s. for a small wooden trolley on rubber wheels. Bids of one and two shillings were made for small chairs, stools, buckets, etc. Crates of hundreds of small bottles went for £1 and less. An electric wall clock sold for £2 10s. and coke stoves fetched £1 and 30s. each.[19]

Jenny Jefferies Remembers

'My father Jim Clothier was the gardener there when Norman Hall owned it. Mr Hall was the owner of Eezalls soap products. I remember going there as a child and having food I had never eaten before in the very large kitchen. The cook was a single lady who was very kind to my sister and myself. I went to stay with her in a flat in Clifton - quite an experience for a child that had never stayed away from home. She used to make fantastic food and ice cream. My Dad used to exhibit flowers from the garden at Bristol Flowers show on the Downs. I remember going there in an Eezalls van with large chrysanthemums wrapped in tissue paper. Unfortunately, I cannot remember the cooks name, but she looked very much like the actress in Downton Abbey.'

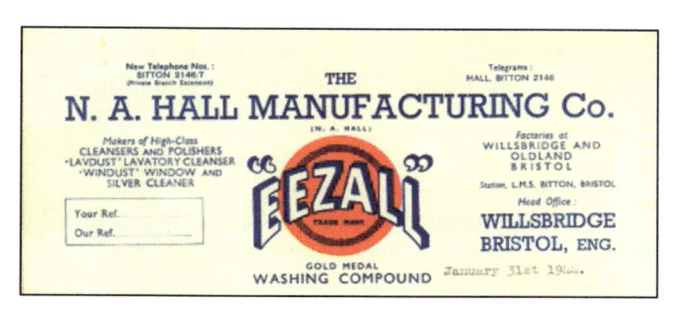

'With Compliments' slip, January 31, 1944
Courtesy Kingswood Museum

Pauline Harris Remembers

'Mr. Hall owned a soap packing factory, Eezall, at the Querns in Willsbridge. He moved to the Lons during the 1940's where he kept numbers of Shire horse which were put out to graze on the land which is now Fonthill Garden Centre. The Halls entertained the local residents with garden parties. For one of these garden parties they hired a pantomime horse to give rides to the children. I have a photograph from a local paper with myself and other children sat on them. '

Pat and Keith Short Remember

'Just a little information about Norman Hall, bearing in mind these are memories of almost 80 years ago so there may be some inaccuracies, for example the number of horses and the dates but Keith has never forgotten being given a half a crown and his obvious pleasure in giving to them.

About the end of the 1930s and early 1940s Norman Hall lived and had a factory at the 'Querns' a large stone-built house opposite the garage in Willsbridge.   Local people worked there filling boxes with his washing powder Eezall.

When he was a boy, my husband Keith remembers going there on a Saturday morning, with his friends to help load the boxes on to a horse drawn trailer, after which they were told to line up and they were given a half a crown each (2 shillings and 6 pence) Also, at Christmas, they would go carol singing there, and were invited in the house, and again, were given a half a crown each.

Norman owned about 10 or 12 horses which were kept at Willsbridge. Some Shire and some show jumping horses. Bert Legge was his jockey, and he was helped in the stables by his brother, and Wally Hemmings, a local man who lived in Cherry Gardens, who, was also a foreman in the factory. It was quite an impressive sight to see the string of horses, saddled up and walking up the road.

They could have been going to a field situated between Bridgeyate and Warmley, which Keith believes Norman owned.   He also had the factory at the bottom of the "Turnpike", Barry Road, Oldland Common and he had a farm in Caerleon, Newport, Wales.'

---

[1] 'Betting Prosecutions in Bristol' *Western Daily Press*, Nov 13, 1902
[2] 'Bristol Estates', *Western Daily Press*, 9 January 1933
[3] Email, Pat Short, 18 August 2020
[4] Email, Marlene Gallop, 23 September 2020
[5] Many Tributes to Norman Abbott Hall', *Somerset Guardian*, 22 March 1974, p.20
[6] Email, Pat Short, 18 August 2020
[7] Many Tributes to Norman Abbott Hall', *Somerset Guardian*, 22 March 1974, p.20
[8] https://historicengland.org.uk/, List Entry Number: 1255451, accessed 23 September 2020
[9] *Keynsham and Saltford Life and Work in Times Past, v.7* ed. Elizabeth White, (Keynsham: Keynsham and Saltford History Society, 1990, p.36)
[10] Many Tributes to Norman Abbott Hall', *Somerset Guardian*, 22 March 1974, p.20
[11] 'Sale of Factory Equipment', *Bristol Evening Post*, 20 August 1953
[12] Email, Pat Short, 18 August 2020
[13] *Keynsham and Saltford Life and Work in Times Past, v.7* ed. Elizabeth White, (Keynsham: Keynsham and Saltford History Society, 1990, p.36)
[14] 'History of Detergents', www.detergentsandsoaps.com/detergents-history.html, accessed 23 September 2020
[15] 'Lord Leverhulme's Ghost: Colonial Exploitation in the Congo' (review), Rich, Jeremy, Johns Hopkins University Press, Volume 10, Number 1, Spring 2009
[16] Email, Marlene Gallop, 23 September 2020
[17] Synthetic Detergents: 100 years of history' https://www.ncbi.nlm.nih.gov/pmc/articles/PMC5605839, accessed 23 September2020
[18] Sale of Factory Equipment', *Bristol Evening Post*, 20 August 1953
[19] 'Howes, Luce, Williams and Payne' Publication unknown, 1953

Chapter 9   Hugh Butler Folliott

From 1953 onwards The Lons underwent exciting changes. Now, not only was it a family home for the Folliott family and the office for a global business; a business which continued the tradition of inventive, innovative entrepreneurs who lived at The Lons, but it was also a school; a school, which is remembered fondly by a number of its former pupils over fifty years later. The school at The Lons had been transferred from Keynsham when the family moved to Bitton.

Hugh Butler Folliott, his wife Frances Carlile Folliott *née* Hale, their five children, Julia, Martin, Anthony, Helena and Louise, together with Hugh's aunt, Minnie Folliott, moved into The Lons in 1953.[1] (Other records give 1951[2] and 1955[3] as the move in date, but 1953 is taken as the definitive one as it comes from Frances Folliott herself.)

So who were Hugh and Frances Folliott?

Photo courtesy of Julia Scott

Hugh Butler Folliott (1910-1968) was one of four children and the son of Harry Folliott (1868-1947) and Ellen Maria Butler (1872-1968). Harry was Secretary to a Public Company[4] and a Chartered accountant and was thought to have been a descendant of one of the Huguenots who had fled France. His family had been in silk weaving. Hugh's mother was a music teacher, a talented pianist, and her sister a violinist[5] which perhaps has some bearing on Hugh's love of music and theatre as an adult.

Hugh spent his childhood in Hackney[6] and Hornsey[7] where he was still living in 1933[8] but by 1934 when he married Frances he had moved to Bristol.[9] He had the job of training and organising the administrative staff for the Totalizator on dog racing tracks around the country. However, when a law suit was brought against Totalizators in general, Hugh decided to leave this employment and he took on an area manager's post with a company which sold women's toiletries[10] before setting up his own business.

Frances Carlile Hale *(1910-1999) was* born on 14th February 1910 in Queensland, Australia.[11] She was the eldest child of an English clergyman, Herbert Percy Hale (1867-1940) and Marie Isobel Carlile Thomas (1882-1948) whose parents had emigrated to Australia before she was born. Herbert attended Oxford University[12] and having been ordained in 1896,[13] he worked for a few years as a clergyman in the north of England before becoming a missionary on the South African railways prior to emigrating to Australia in 1908.[14] Marie, having set up a school in Sydney, travelled to America to work supporting the Principal of a school in Chicago before returning to Australia via England. It was on the voyage to Australia that Herbert and Marie met. A year later in 1909 the couple married in Hunters Hill, New South Wales[15] and their first child, Frances, was born a year later followed by her brother Reggie.

By 1911 Herbert was on the electoral roll in Australia having been responsible for parishes in Boonah (a'bush' parish) and Wynnum. Both Herbert and Marie had kept strong links with their extended families in England and in 1914 they returned to England – partly for health reasons and partly for the education of their children. Herbert became the vicar at Hartington, Derbyshire and Frances was brought up in the rectory and experienced an education along the PNEU lines which, as we will see later, she was to provide for others when adult. Herbert became a field chaplain in France for the Church Army in the first world war[16] – the Church Army having been set up by a relative. In 1916 Frances' sister, Ursula, was born,[17] and a year later the family moved to St Peter's Rectory, Nottingham where Herbert became rector.

Engagement photo for Hugh and Frances

'In 1932 everyone who put their engagement in the Times was flooded with offers of free photographs. If the announcement was the birth of a daughter one got a mass of amusing literature. The one I liked best was an insurance to cover the expenses of your daughter's presentation at Court.'

Photo and text courtesy of Julia Scott from 'Talking to my Five Children – Frances Folliott' by Julia Scott

Hugh and Frances met at a dance in Belgium in 1928 when they were both on holiday touring the battlefields from the First World War.[18] At the time Frances enjoyed the company of Hugh's brother Geoffrey and hardly noticed Hugh. Geoffrey moved to Malaya and Frances had occasional correspondence with him. Four years later the shy, retiring Hugh made a surprise visit to Frances' house and over the next couple of years the couple went on various outings together before becoming engaged and marrying in 1934.

Marriage certificate for Hugh Butler Folliott and Frances Carlile Hale

The Marriage of Hugh and Frances

Hugh and Frances married at Christchurch, Woking, Surrey on October 6th 1934. Frances' father officiated at the ceremony. The reception, with around 80 guests, was at Kilworth (Frances was the great niece of Sir Thomas and Lady Cave of Kilworth).

Newspapers described it as *'a fashionable wedding at Woking' 'interesting and picturesque'* with the *'interior of the church decorated for the harvest festival.'*

The honeymoon was at Avoncliffe, Bradford on Avon
Photo courtesy Julia Scott

Following their marriage, the couple lived in Chewton Keynsham. The house required a lot of work and had a large garden which included bees, chickens and a market garden.

The house at Chewton Keynsham
photo courtesy of Julia Scott

Hugh set up The Butler Trading Company which marketed patents and, although money was very short and the company not overly profitable, Hugh remained a company director in the domestic patent market[19] until the start of the war. His daughter, Julia Scott, recalls him driving from central Bristol to Chewton and back in order to have lunch, and all in an hour! He also had to travel with his patented products which included self-locking household and platform steps, ironing tables, garden chairs and draught excluders. By the time war broke out he was working on a patent sewage purifier for the government to use in camps.

Whilst at Chewton Hugh and Frances took part in community life and were members of Whittucks Amateur Dramatic Society which performed at the Charlton Cinema in Keynsham. Although they did not have leading roles, the critics described their performances from 1938 as follows: *'Mrs H.B.Folliott played convincingly as the plastic Mrs Blake and Mr Hugh Folliott gave an attractive study of the ship's commander...'*[20] This enjoyment of amateur dramatics was to be seen later in the school curriculum which Frances delivered at The Gateway School at The Lons. They were also keen tennis players and Frances spent a lot of time working in the large garden.

The 1939 register shows the family were still living in Chewton Keynsham.[21] Hugh was an army reservist who had been called up for training. However, a family memoir says that he applied to the Air Force but at 29 he was considered too old! By 1940 he was commissioned to second lieutenant in the Royal Regiment of Artillery[22] and was training in Bulford before being attached to the 51st Highland Field Regiment. By 1942 he was part of the regular army emergency commissions working in military intelligence.[23] He was abroad for much of the war serving in Ireland, France,

Kenya (where he climbed Kilimanjaro), and was promoted to Major in Ranchi when the war came to an end. It was not until February 1946 that he returned to his family.

July 15th 1940 2nd Lt. H Folliott RA
When first commissioned these pictures taken free.

Photos courtesy of Julia Scott

With Hugh serving in the army money was tight and Frances decided to rent out the Chewton Keynsham house. She moved with the children to a PNEU school, St John's, Green Hammerton, York where she worked as a teacher for four years.

PNEU schools or Parents National Educational Union schools were originally set up in 1887 to support parents with home schooling and were based on the ideas of Charlotte Mason (1842-1923). A number of schools across the country were opened as PNEU schools which followed the ideology and principles expounded by Charlotte Mason. Charlotte Mason believed in a wide and liberal curriculum that was securely founded on the teachings from the Bible. Her motto for children was 'I am, I can; I ought, I will'.[24] She thought it important to educate not just the mind but the whole person. Education was 'an atmosphere, a discipline, a life'. Atmosphere referred to the child's environment; discipline to the cultivation of good habits and good character; life to intellectual and academic pursuits.[25]

The PNEU Badge and Motto

The bird is a skylark soaring high into the sky.

This represents the ability of everyone to rise to great heights and to stay there.

Our motto is: I am, I can, I ought, I will.

I am – each of us is a person in our own right and has within us the power of knowing ourselves, both our qualities and our faults.

I can – we have the ability to use our talents to the full and should never be tempted to waste them through lack of effort.

I ought – our own conscience and knowledge of right and wrong tell us what we ought to do and we should all do our best to see that we carry this out.

I will – a determination on our part to listen to our conscience and to act on what we ought to do.

Charlotte Mason: photo courtesy of Wikipedia and in the public domain

The education Charlotte Mason advocated sounds progressive for the end of the nineteenth century. She believed in 'living' textbooks by which she meant books which used stories and pictures to convey facts, children were expected to keep a nature journal and there was a focus on music, art and literature. The Folliotts' commitment to this philosophy, which both the Keynsham and Lons schools were founded on, can be seen clearly in the memories of Sarah Perrett and Caroline Martin at the end of this section. Both girls attended the school at The Lons and write of nature walks, picture study, beautifully illustrated books which they have kept all these years, ballet and drama productions. The school also offered support for children unable to write quickly in exams with parents coming to school to act as scribes.

Charlotte Mason's methods are still used by some parents who home school today and Fairfield Independent School at Backwell, Bristol is currently run as a PNEU school. Further details about Charlotte Mason's educational philosophy can be found on their website.[26]

Frances and the children returned to Keynsham to live with her parents prior to moving back into the Chewton Keynsham house. The family were very shocked by the damage which the tenants had done and they had much work to do when they returned to the house.

Frances' parents were still living in Keynsham when, in 1940 and 1948 Frances' father[27] and mother[28] died. Hugh's father died in 1947 so the first decade of married life was not without sadness for the family. This was intensified with Hugh's war work taking him away from the family for the duration of the war.[29]

Immediately after the second world war, Frances Folliott ran a small school for two or three pupils in the Chewton house. By the end of the 1940s she had expanded this and was headteacher of a PNEU school for primary children in one of the barns adjacent to Rockhill House, Keynsham.[30] Frances had attended The Charlotte Mason Teacher Training College in Ambleside for two years. She then worked as a governess, as a teacher in a PNEU school and for a short time in a school for the deaf. She was clearly well prepared for the venture of setting up her own school.[31]

The Lons around the time it was a school in the 1950s: photo courtesy of David Noble

The move to The Lons was brought about by the couple's wish to expand the school. So, in the early 1950s Hugh and Frances together with their five children (age range approximately seven to seventeen) and Hugh's Aunt Minnie moved into The Lons and set up The Gateway School. Nevertheless the older children would have spent limited time at The Lons as they were away for boarding school, college, National Service and travel.

The Folliott family at The Lons 1954 and 1955
Photos courtesy of Julia Scott

Minnie Folliott *(1870-1968)* had never married but had spent some of her life working as a governess, both as a live-in for a clerical family in Derbyshire and as a private day governess in London before becoming a lady's companion. She then moved to Bath. Her experience as a governess would be apt for someone living with her nephew and his family in a school and it may have been partly due to this experience that she was able to build up a good rapport with the children at the school, who enjoyed serving her lunch. Sarah, in her memories below, describes her as 'lovely'.

Cold Time to Move

ABOUT 40 boarders at a private school at BITTON have found themselves thrust into a country winter after a long sojourn at KEYNSHAM.

They have just moved from the Somerset town to The Lons, Bath Road, Bitton, former home of Mr. and Mrs. N. A. Hall. The 19th-century mansion has been converted into The Gateway Parents' National Education Union School.

The school stands in its own grounds and has more than 18 rooms. Extensive alterations have been made in the last few months to make classrooms, cloakrooms and more windows.

The Gateway's former home was at Wellsway, Keynsham, but shortage of accommodation necessitated a change.

The principal, Mrs. F. C. Folliatt, told me: "I know the winter is a bad time to move a school, but we had to take the immediate opportunity. Everyone is settling down nicely, although the weather did cause us a little bother."

THE GATEWAY SCHOOL
(P.N.E.U.)

BITTON, BRISTOL   Tel.: Bitton 2130

BOARDING & DAY SCHOOL for Girls 4—12 and Boys 4—9 years.

Only a limited number of Boarders are taken in order to keep a personal family atmosphere. A School 'bus'—for which NO CHARGE is made—collects pupils from BATH, SALTFORD, KEYNSHAM and District.

Prospectus and full particulars may be obtained from the Principal, Mrs. H. B. Folliott, C.M.C.

Photos of 'Cold Time to Move' and The Gateway School courtesy of Julia Scott.

THE GATEWAY P.N.E.U. SCHOOL
(Prop.: H. B. FOLLIOTT)

THE LONS, BITTON
GLOUCESTERSHIRE

Principal: Mrs. H. B. FOLLIOTT
(Charlotte Mason College)

Telephone: Bitton 2130

HOURS OF WORK

Morning—9.15 a.m. to 12.45 p.m. (with interval for play and drill).

Afternoon—1.45 p.m. to 3.30 p.m.

No school on Saturday.

UNIFORM

Sole Suppliers—The Don, Bath.

P.N.E.U. ties, badges, ribbons, snake belts, are obtainable from the school.

One pair of house shoes or gym shoes to be kept at school.

"THE LONS" is a modernised country residence standing in its own grounds of 10 acres and situated 6 miles from Bath or Bristol.

Buses from Bath, Bristol, Keynsham, Warmley, Kingswood and Hanham stop at the entrance drive.

Our own school bus collects and delivers at no charge, in Saltford, Keynsham and Bath.

The Gateway School is closely associated with the Parents' National Educational Union (P.N.E.U.), and the Programmes of the Parents' Union School (P.U.S.) are followed in all the Forms.

The aim of the school is to carry out the principles of Charlotte Mason and to give its pupils an education which embraces mental, moral and physical development.

Early training in habits of industry, concentration, and observation, in the power of self-expression and the use of controlled imagination is considered of utmost importance if a child is to develop to the best of his or her ability.

The school is for girls from 4 to 12 years of age and boys from 4 to 9 years of age. Girls are prepared for Secondary and Public Schools— Boys for Preparatory Schools. The size of the classes is limited to ensure that every child receives individual attention. The staff are all qualified teachers.

Curriculum includes Scripture, Literature, Reading, Writing, Grammar, History, Citizenship, French, Mathematics, Geography, Natural History, Nature Painting, Nature Walks, Picture Study, Drawing, Handwork and Singing.

Games—Rounders and net-ball.

FEES

Tuition only

Nursery Class (4 to 5 years) mornings only. 9 guineas per term plus fee for each morning's attendance.

Under 6 years	22½ guineas per term
Under 7 years	24½ " " "
Over 7 and under 9 years	27½ " " "
Over 9 years	30½ " " "

Board only

Termly
Weekly

A reduction is made for two or more children of the same family.

Dinners (Day pupils) ... £7.15.– per term
"Elevenses" ... 7.6. " "

Optional Extras

Dancing ... 3½ guineas per term
Piano ... 4½ " " "
Swimming (Summer Term) ...

Fees are payable in advance. A term's notice or the equivalent fee is required before a child is removed.

Fees are not remitted on account of absence, but parents can avail themselves of the School Fees Remission Scheme, particulars of which can be obtained from the school.

The Headmistress reserves the right of requiring a pupil to be withdrawn for any cause she may deem reasonable.

In cases of absence, a note of explanation is requested from the parents.

A section from the school prospectus, date unknown. Photo courtesy Julia Scott

The Lons offered a lot more space both indoors and outside – outdoor activities being very important for PNEU schools – and it would also allow them to take a few pupils as boarders in the early years although in the later years they only catered for day pupils. Nevertheless if the parents of these pupils were away then the children would stay at The Lons for a night or two. Local children were picked up from Upton Cheyney and surrounding villages by dormobile.

Gateway PNEU School photo - 81 pupils, 11 staff. Date not known

Photo courtesy of Julia Scott

Photo courtesy of Julia Scott

1964

Miss Hunt Miss Taylor Miss Aldridge Mrs Lawrence Miss Catling Mrs Folliott
Miss Fox Mrs Towler Mrs Currie Mrs Hendy Mrs Densley

Photo courtesy of Julia Scott

Form 2 with Mrs Folliott, Miss Fox, Miss Ozanne and Miss Catling 1960

H Self   D Dolling   L Folliott   M Oscroft   B King-Smith   J McQueen   R Lush

Photos courtesy of Julia Scott

Drama was a key component of the school curriculum and there was an annual production by Muriel Catling (both a teacher and friend of the Folliotts). There was a range of plays from 'The Tempest' to 'The Sleeping Beauty'. All the costumes were made by Frances Folliott and the memories below give a sense of the excitement the productions produced.

1960 - THE TEMPEST

The school was clearly a happy place as can be seen from the memories at the end of this section which reveal a genuine warmth and affection for the school. As previously stated the school followed a PNEU curriculum and from reading her memories it is clear that Frances Folliott was passionate about this. Being small, around 60 – 70 pupils in 1962, contributed to the school's family atmosphere. For example, children chose the lunchtime pudding on their birthdays and took lunch to 'Mr Folliott's mother'. Lunch was actually taken to Hugh Folliott's Aunt Minnie. Hugh's mother, Ellen Maria Butler Folliott, continued to live in Haringey until her death in 1968.[32] Minnie was living at The Lons from 1955 until her death in 1968 having reached the grand age of 97, it is very credible that she would have been bedridden with the 'huge card' produced for a birthday when she was well into her nineties. Staff became family friends, some of them living in and as can be seen in the photo below their celebrations became family celebrations.

95

Jennifer Elphicks 21ˢᵗ Birthday - she was one of the school's live in student teachers. The photo was taken in the drawing room. Far right is Jessie Taylor, the school's matron. Right is boarders' craft time which took place in the drawing room: photos courtesy Julia Scott

Boarders' bedroom Photos courtesy of Julia Scott

No doubt some work was required to convert the building into a school and living quarters for the family, but to date there is no knowledge of what this entailed. Frances describes it as *'an adventure'*[33] The house was cold with little in the way of heating. There was a temperamental boiler in the cellar and a few radiators, but oil heaters, electric fires and warm clothing were the order of the day. However a few details of changes which had taken place over the previous fifty years can be glimpsed from Sarah and Caroline's memories. They write of playing netball on the tennis court at Bitton Hill which suggests that there were no longer tennis courts at The Lons, although we know that tennis was a favourite pastime for Hugh and Frances and the family continued to play tennis at The Lons. The rec was used for sport so maybe the gardens remained in a formal state. However the gravel terrace leading down to the lawn which can be seen in many photos was used by the children at playtimes.

The family kept hens and pigs and needed help with these as well as the garden. Consequently they put a residential caravan in the garden for the Harker family to live in.[34]

Photos courtesy of Julia Scott

By 1968 Hugh was experiencing some health issues and Frances felt that it was time for her to retire. Consequently the school closed in 1968 and its end was marked by a garden party and pageant with around 350 guests to celebrate 100 years of The Lons building. There was a series of mimes suggesting different time periods in the house's lifetime and a huge cake with a hundred candles. Frances Folliott spoke about the importance of parents and school working together with school being 'the junior partner'.

Pupils say farewell in grand style

A HUGE cake, blazing with 100 candles was the centre of a tableau which brought tears to many people's eyes.

The cake was to celebrate the centenary of The Lions, the home of the Gateway P.N.E.U. School in Bitton.

But the occasion was not all celebration. For the school was closing down after 17 years.

And it closed in style.

About 300 parents and former pupils came to the last summer entertainment at the school, a garden party and pageant.

Acted by present and past pupils, the pageant depicted the events of the last 100 years.

Excerpts from the first school play productions were put on and scenes from the days of the Suffragettes, the Great War and the Second World War were mimed.

All the songs of those years were sung which made the scenes realistic. These included "It's a long way to Tipperary," "The Bells Are Ringing" and "Pack Up All My Cares and Woe."

And at the end the huge cake was cut and slices were passed round.

The ballet was arranged and produced by Mrs. D. Woods and Mrs. W. Williams was the accompanist.

The series of mimes and

Janice Smith, Emma Seymour-Williams and Pamela Burrows, dressed in period costume, had the right setting of the 100-year-old house for their pageant.

acts "I Recollect" was written by Miss Muriel Catling. The music was arranged by Mrs. W. Williams.

At the prizegiving Headmistress, Mrs. Folliott, spoke of the aims and work of the school during the past 17 years and paid tribute to the dedicated work of the staff.

Presentation of prizes

Arithmetic Shield (presented by Parents' Association).—Senior: Sarah Perrett. Junior: David Walker.

Dancing Cup.—(Presented by A. Somerset): Sara Harapath.

Drama Cup.—(Presented by D. Hammett): Anne Richards.

Art Cup.—(Presented by W. Luscombe): Emma Jane Seymour Williams.

English Cup.—(Presented by S. Arengo): Catherine Barrett.

Writing Cup.—(Presented by M. Vine): 7/8 years: A. Seymour Williams, 5/6 years: P. Drewatt.

Spelling Cup.—(Presented by R. Dalwood): Senior: K. Howard. Junior: K. Wilcox.

French Cup.—(Presented by Mrs. Folliott): Anne Richards.

Senior Endeavour Cup.—(Presented by E. J. Richards): Julie Hawkins.

Junior Endeavour Cup.—(Presented by S. Lexx Bagg): Jonathan Bowse.

Music Cup.—(Presented by Mrs. Folliott): Sarah Perrett.

Swimming Cup.—(Presented by A. Perretti: Sarah Perrett.

Swimming Certificates 100 yards: K. Howard, A. Richards, E. Seymour Williams, K. Wilcox, D. Cobbold.

Dancing Certificates Examination taken July 13. Grade I: A. Seymour Williams (Pass); A. Kifner (pass); J. Baron, T. Hall, K. Smith (pass commended). Grade II: S. Herapath, J. Hawkins (pass commended) E. J. Seymour Williams, K. Howard, J. Russett (pass). Grade III: A. Richards, C. Parrell, S. Perrett (all pass commended). Grade I: Cecchetti: J. Hawkins.

Beverley Alber gets a ride in a wheelbarrow from her friends who took part in the pageant.

Frances Folliott was the headteacher and ran the school. Meanwhile Hugh was engaged in other business interests and inventions, of which his daughter, Julia, says there were many. For a few years he spent some time working for Kenwood in Woking during the week only returning to The Lons at weekends.[35] Kenwoods bought the rights for Hugh's toaster timer and Julia remembers that 'The Lons used to be full of toast being tested because toasting is complicated by water content etc.' He had been a merchant[36] and director of a patent company[37] and he was working on these other ideas as well as his Vermipeat invention before he set up the Vermipeat business in 1963.[38] Vermipeat, as will be seen later, was an innovative idea which gained worldwide success.

Presentation to Mrs Folliott

Julia Scott née Folliott reminisces on her childhood in her book *Letters From Freetown:*

'It was a happy childhood. My parents saw their life together as an exciting adventure and felt their children were dragged behind their chariot wheels and must judge how much they enjoyed it. Mum called my father a 'Romantic Adventurer' – his adventures taking the form of invention and new businesses which often struggled. Mum gave stability by teaching and running a popular junior school which included boarders so there was always a large 'family'.

A few years after settling into The Lons the children began to move away. Travel was important to the family. In 1958, aged 21, Anthony Flexon Folliott decided to travel and left the family home for Malaysia to work as a planter on a rubber plantation. He gave his last permanent address as The Lons, Bitton and gave Malaya as his intended permanent future residence.[39] Anthony was not travelling entirely into the unknown as his uncle, Geoffrey Butler Folliott (1907-1979) had been living there before moving to Australia. (Geoffrey had emigrated with his family ten years earlier.[40] Geoffrey had been a police superintendant there.)[41] Although mainly working on the plantations, Anthony also worked in conjunction with the world bank and fuller details of his time in Malaysia can be found in *Tony's Memoirs of his time in Malaysia and Indonesia by Julia Scott*. Although he returned to England for a few years to run Vermipeat after his father's death, he then left to live in Australia.

Travel remained important to other younger members of the family, since two years later Martin, aged 20, travelled to New York City from Amsterdam on the Seven Seas airline.[42] However he did not do the more extensive travelling that other siblings engaged in and gave his permanent address as The Lons. In 1959 Julia took a four week voyage to Australia on the £10.00 pommie scheme. She was away for several years and visited New Zealand, Malaya, Bangkok, Calcutta, Delhi, Turkey and

Tehran.[43] She worked for one year in Tasmania and one year in Brisbane. In 1965 she went to Sierra Leone for two years as a VSO (Voluntary Service Overseas).[44] Here she set up an Occupational Therapy Department in the psychiatric hospital there. It was in Sierra Leone that she met her future husband. Helena R.S. Folliott also travelled aged 20. She went to New York City when in transit to an alternative destination – probably to Canada where she worked as a teacher for many years.[45] Marriage also followed for most of the children in the 1960s and 70s. Julia married John A. Scott, Louise married Peter Cawthra, Martin married Penelope Knowles and Helena married John Tutcho. Both Julia and Louise had wedding receptions at The Lons.

Met in Sierra Leone, married at Keynsham

A COUPLE who met in Sierra Leone were married in Victoria Methodist Church, Keynsham, on Saturday.

The bride was Miss Julia Carlile Folliott, eldest daughter of Mr and Mrs H. B. Folliott, of The Lons, Bitton, and the bridegroom Mr John Scott, only son of Mr and Mrs J. Scott, of Beckenham, Kent.

The bride, who has just returned from pioneering occupational therapy in a mental hospital in Sierra Leone, was for several years head of the occupational therapy department at Frenchay Hospital. She has also worked in Tasmania, Australia and New Zealand.

The bridegroom is a director of J. Leete and Co. and met the bride while organising the transport of £2m worth of machinery up country to the diamond mines in Sierra Leone.

Previous to joining the company he was a captain in the American Merchant Navy.

The service was conducted by the Rev N. Skinner, assisted by the Rev A. Cox, of St John's Church, Keynsham.

The bride wore a sheath dress of deep cream Italian silk with a matching ribbon lace train. Her veil was worn by her great-grandmother exactly 100 years ago.

The bridesmaid, Miss Louise Folliott, wore a dress of brown wild silk and cream lace.

The bride's second sister, Miss Helena Folliott, flew from Cambridge Bay, North West Territory, Canada, where she has been teaching Eskimoes for two years.

A pre-wedding reception was held last Friday evening and after the ceremony the wedding breakfast was attended by relatives and close friends of the two families at The Lons, Bitton.

The honeymoon is being spent in Morocco and the couple will live at Meopham, Kent.

Photo courtesy of Julia Scott

The year 1963 was the start of Hugh Folliott's Vermipeat business. Hugh had invented an all-purpose compost, Vermipeat. He combined this with other products including Vermipeat Readi-pots.[46]

Mr. H. B. Folliott, the managing director, Mr. R. Barnes, the factory manager, and Mrs. M. Smith, the forewoman, look on as Miss E. Ball operates a machine producing 3,000 plant pots an hour at a Saltford factory.

Vermipeat was a mixture of vermiculite, peat and slow release fertiliser. This produced a sponge like substance which resembled polystyrene in appearance. It was originally manufactured as a fertiliser but was then also used for other related products. One of these was Vermipeat Readi-pots.

The Vermipeat was moulded into the shape of a plant pot which then had the advantage of being soil-less yet enabling seedlings to grow.

Photo from Bristol Evening Post March 1st 1967

Hugh worked on his Vermipeat invention in a workshop he had made in the attic of The Lons and began production in an old barn in Westerleigh near Yate.[47] In 1963 he bought an old mill building adjacent to The Jolly Sailor in Mead Lane Saltford. Here he set up the manufacture and marketing of Vermipeat. The business achieved some considerable success and sold around forty to fifty million pots in its first three years. It quickly became a global enterprise and when Hugh looked to find a market in America he soon received an initial order for ten million pots to launch in fourteen U.S. cities. This was followed by large orders (3-5 million) from a number of individual growers. The vermiculite was imported from America and Hugh was not slow to see the irony in this. In an interview for a newspaper he said, *'it really amazes me, especially when you think it's the States where I get the vermiculite.'* [48] However, he held the British and American patents so was the one with a monopoly on the product. The pots were in much demand around the world, including places such as Trinidad, Barbados, Greenland and Israel. They were suitable for growing a wide variety of plants which included Channel Island tomatoes, African sugar cane and Malaysian rubber plants. Such was the demand for the product that Hugh decided to build a warehouse and factory for further expansion of the business and easier export of product through Avonmouth Docks.[49]

In the mid-1960s life at The Lons appeared to be going well. The school was successful and the Vermipeat business was expanding rapidly. There is some oral evidence that Hugh frequently travelled abroad in connection with his Vermipeat business.

Vermipeat after Hugh Butler Folliott's death
After Hugh's death in 1969, Anthony returned from abroad to run the business and Martin took leave of absence from his school. Much of the credit for keeping Vermipeat going and eventually paying off all debts is due to Martin and Tony. A couple of years later he was joined by his sister Julia Scott and her husband John. In 1974 Anthony moved to Australia and John Scott was sole director. The Saltford factory was closed in 1984 when it was taken over by Silverperl. John and Julia continued to work for Silverperl until it moved to Lincoln when they bought the sole rights to Vermipeat compost amongst other products and set up their own horticultural business.

Image and information from Saltford Environment Group

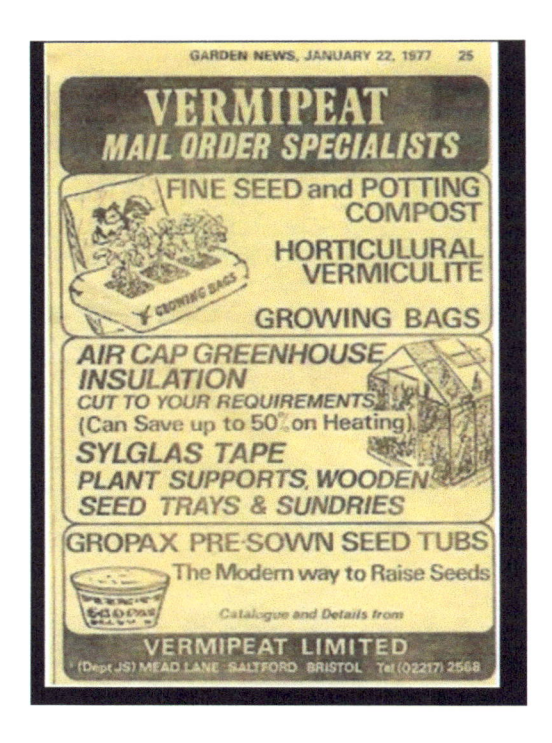

The church continued to be a focus for the family and at times they had missionaries from St John's Church, Keynsham staying with them at The Lons. When Hugh died a chalice and paten were consecrated at St John's Church in his memory. The couple also rented the school to the brownies on at least one occasion. The Lons would have been a busy place when they lived there and full of people. The 1965 electoral roll for The Lons, Bitton shows that as well as Hugh, Frances, Julia, Martin and Minnie, Marilyn Bradshaw, Hugh Folliott's secretary, Mary Hunt, a student teacher and Jessie F. Taylor, the school's matron were living there.

Photos courtesy of Julia Scott

Perhaps this is also 1961/62 with all the family. Note the School van in the back.

At some point while the family were living at The Lons some of the grounds were sold to Fonthill Garden Centre. Hugh Folliott also applied for planning permission to build some houses and flats but permission was not granted.[50] It was a bone of contention that planning permission had been given to the next owners of The Lons since the building works were to provide Hugh and Frances with a pension pot. This would have been particularly useful since, following delivery issues with Canadian Vermiculite, Hugh and Frances were forced to take a mortgage on The Lons to finance this.[51]

1968 did not begin well for the family. Minnie died, aged 97, on 28th January of that year. Four months later on 17th May, Ellen Maria Folliott, Hugh's mother, died in Haringey, London, aged 96.

```
FOLLIOTT Ellen Maria of 62 Woodside Av Highgate London
     died 17 May 1968 Probate London 12 July.  £30623.


FOLLIOTT Minnie of The Lons Bitton Glos died 26 January
     1968 Probate Bristol 27 March.  £3749.
```

Probate records show Hugh's mother and aunt listed one below the other in 1968.

It was also the year the school closed as mentioned previously. This however was a celebrated event which several ex-pupils of the school remember vividly. Nevertheless Hugh's health was failing and a year later Hugh Butler Folliott died in Southmead Hospital. He was buried in St Mary's churchyard, Bitton.

```
FOLLIOTT Hugh Butler of The Lons Bitton nr Bristol died
     13 August 1969 Administration (with Will) Bristol
     10 December.  £20314.
```

Name.	Abode.	When buried.	Age.	By whom the Ceremony was performed.
Hugh Butler Folliott No. 2745.	The Lons Bitton (died at Southmead Hospital)	15th August 1969	59	N.R.E Jacks Curate of Keynsham

Following Hugh Folliott's death in December 1969, Roger Fowler, the owner of GS Cars, Tower Road, Warmley sold a car to A.F.Folliott i.e. Anthony. Roger remembers it as a rather interesting vehicle. It was a blue Gilbern Genie, sold both in kit form and assembled. Whilst Roger is not sure whether Anthony bought the kit or assembled form, Julia Scott confirmed it was the kit form and Tony was very proud of it. The Gilbern Genie was produced in Llantwit Fardre, Pontypridd and in 1969 would have cost about £2,000[52] so would have been 'an enviable acquisition'. Anthony tried to sell the car back to GS Cars in 1973, presumably this was when he was leaving the country for Australia. Roger declined to buy the car and does not know what happened to this exclusive vehicle.

August 1972. Frances at The Lons and chalice and Paten in memory of Hugh Folliott, at St John's Church, Keynsham. *Photos courtesy Julia Scott*

Frances remained at The Lons for a few years after Hugh's death. She then moved to Partis College, Newbridge, Bath before spending her final years in St Phillips Residential Home in Keynsham. She died in 1999. However the legacy of Hugh and Frances Folliott lives on in the books written by Julia Scott and no doubt some of their grandchildren will have taken up business pursuits and travel.

Hugh and Frances Folliott – Lons Drawing Room 1966
Photo from Talking to My Children – Frances Folliott courtesy of Julia Scott

Some of my more personal memories of living in The Lons by Louise Cawthra née Folliott

My childhood memories of living at the Lons started when we moved there, aged 6 years. From the age of 11-16 I was at a PNEU boarding school in Berkshire, so home at the holidays, then for 2 years 1963 -5 I lived at 'home' before starting my nursing training.

For me it was a very happy uncomplicated young childhood, the house was large (well enormous to me!), it was always full of people other than immediate family - there was the matron/organising the boarders etc, usually a student teacher, a teacher, father's secretary too (often with their own children) - we had plenty of space to play in, the garden with a large terrace in front of the house and a big bank to roll down onto the large lawn area surrounded by large trees, like the Wellingtonia Tree, a big Cedar tree overhanging a quaint Summer house (good for summer sleepovers and being a play house, when younger), and a Monkey Puzzle tree to name a few - beyond was the field and a tennis court that never quite got finished. The greenhouse and kitchen gardens were always full of goodies - I especially loved eating the grapes which seemed to be plentiful - we had orchards with apple, pear and plum trees, and at the back orchard lots of Hazel trees. The stables down the drive were mainly used for housing chickens, and great place to explore - what wasn't there to like?!!

I was treated like a boarder during term time - about 8-10 of us initially, many children had parents living abroad so often did not go home during the short holidays, I think I was expected to make any newcomers welcome - not always easy, however it made for lots of readymade friends! Schooldays are slightly hazy - loved the art History, with wonderful picture books, we learnt lots of crafts like basket weaving, puppet making, knitting and sewing, history, geography, maths, language and English were all important too, with exams in the summer - when I was older I remember helping the younger children with writing their answers down for them in exams. I remember fondly Miss Catling's exuberance and energy for putting on a Summer Play - sometimes Shakespeare, others were her own productions - my mother used to spend long evenings at the sewing machine making all the costumes! Nature walks were a joy, and I still remember the names of most wild flowers and trees, as do the friends I am still in contact with from those formative school years.

My father loved the idea of being a 'smallholder', so from always having had a few free-range chickens, he built two big 'deep litter' hen houses for ?500+ chickens, on the back orchards - it was frequently my job to feed, water, collect the eggs, and then joint family tasks of cleaning the eggs to go to the weekly wholesaler -ugh!! We also had a number of pigs down in the field, excitement and sometimes trauma when they littered - but I did like the piglets!

Christmastime was always extra special - the house was transformed, a BIG tree and decorations in the hall, classrooms became bedrooms, the 'assembly room' the dining room. Usually there were about 18-20 of us, with brothers and sisters home, aunts, uncles, cousins, and friend or two - all staying for several days. Evenings were spent after dinner in the Drawing room with Granny playing on the grand piano - Chopin her favourite - and my aunt often accompanying her, singing. Boxing day, the whole family and other local families went to the Recreation Ground and played a hockey match - always competitive!

The cellar was used for occasional parties - memorable was Halloween, made definitely spooky!! The coal and coke was kept down there too - I used to hate having to go down there and fill the hods for the Aga and boiler, a daily chore.

A lasting memory must be our driveway, the bane of our lives being full of potholes!! Our visitors dreaded it, especially if they had fancy cars and boyfriends with sporty cars - I think my father felt it a challenge!

The Lons also will be so extra special for being the place for my wedding reception in 1969. It was only a few weeks after my father had died unexpectedly; but it was a lovely occasion with ALL the family and relatives, coming together from different parts of the world, and being able to celebrate with many others on a lovely warm September day.

*The Wedding of Louise Folliott and Peter Cawthra at The Lons in 1969:
photo courtesy of Louise Cawthra and Julia Scott*

Memories of The Lons as a School
The Lons P.N.E.U. school by Sarah Perrett with some input by Anne Coleborn née Richards and Katharine Webbe née Richards

I do not know when the Lons was built but in 1968 we did a pageant for our school play which was covering events in the last 100 years and I am pretty sure that was to celebrate the age of the Lons.

The school was a primary school run by Mrs Folliott. The Lons was also her and her husband's home. Mr Folliott also had his office there for his business called Vermipeat. They moved there in 1951 and I think from Googling it that both the school and the Vermipeat business had been started in Saltford.

There were about 50 pupils. While I was there, there were also 3 boarders whose parents lived abroad. Both the Richards and ourselves boarded there on occasions when our parents went away.

The pupils ranged in age from 4 – 11 but the boys mostly left to go to Middle school, so when I was there for the ages 8 -11, it was only girls.

There was quite a lot of speech and drama taught. We had to take part in the North Somerset festival which involved learning a poem by heart and reciting it in front of a panel of judges and hundreds of other school children at the Guildhall in Bath. Terrifying!

We also put on a school play every year which was written by our teachers and Mrs Folliott would make all the costumes. As every child took part this was amazing as a lot of the costumes were fantastic. We were able to keep them (buy them) afterwards for our dressing up boxes.

Our school play in 1967 where we did the story of Prince Bladud. At the back is Caroline Withers playing King Hudebras and I am in front of her as the Queen. As you can see the costumes are wonderful. Ruth was supposed to appear in that play as one of the pigs that Prince Bladud was looking after, but screamed blue murder when they tried to put her 'head' on (which was just a pig mask). My mother could hear her from the audience and had to go backstage and sort her out, so Ruth never appeared as a pig!

Photo courtesy of Sarah Perrett

Tuesday afternoons were set aside for ballet for the girls. We were taught by Mrs Woods who used to live in Upton Cheyney. We not only learned the basics of ballet and took various exams but also learned some useful dances like the Polka and the Highland Fling. I can still polka but being tall I was always the 'man' so I cannot dance it the correct way round. I am not sure what the boys did on Tuesday afternoons!

Games lessons mostly involved walking in crocodile down to the Rec and playing football. Sometimes we did a few athletics like long jump and high jump – as there is no long jump sand pit there we had to jump onto a blanket which did not really encourage you to put a lot of effort into it. We also played netball on the tennis court up at Bitton Hill. We were transported there in an old school bus which I think was an adapted Bedford van. This was also used to pick up and take home the children who came from the Saltford/Keynsham/Willsbridge direction. I can also remember that we were taken swimming at Hotwells in Bristol – a great treat as we were allowed to take some tuck to eat afterwards.

We quite often went on nature walks, mostly up the fields at the back of the Lons and then down Ryedown Lane. We used to scramble around the old quarry, which no-one thought too dangerous in those days!

We also did Picture study where we had a beautiful cardboard covered book which had the biography of a famous artist and several lovely colour plates of the main well-known pictures. We kept these at the end of the school year and I still have those books today!

In front of the school was a gravel terrace then a slope down to a huge lawn. If it was too wet to play on the grass we were confined to the terrace. At the bottom of the lawn there was an enormous tree,– possibly something like a cedar tree, that had a very long rope with a knot in the end, hanging from a branch, that we could swing on. I seem to remember you swung over a fairly large drop which had the fence to the field next door in it so it might have been a Ha-Ha at some stage?

The Lons. Photo taken at the time when it was a school and when Sarah Perrett, Anne Richards, Katharine Richards and Caroline Withers attended.
Photo courtesy of Sarah Perrett

We all had exams every year except the very youngest children. For the first couple of years, when we would have been too slow at writing them ourselves, we had parents come in and take down our answers as dictation – unfortunately, you were not allowed to have your own parent writing your answers so again it was pretty scary.

There were some wonderful traditions that you would only get in a small school like that. If it was your birthday you were allowed to choose what pudding we had at lunchtime. Most people chose ice cream and jelly or chocolate crisp with pink blancmange but I think it was Anne (Perrett) who upset everyone one year by choosing rice pudding!

Mr Folliott's mother also lived at the Lons although she was bedridden. She reached her 100th birthday and we made a huge card with pictures of some of the inventions that occurred in her lifetime. When you were in the top class (which was actually the last 3 years all together) you had to take it in turns to take up her lunch on a tray. She was lovely and if you were lucky you got a sweet. Being a big house that used to have a main staircase and a back staircase this was one of the few occasions one got to go up the main stairs.

Jessie Taylor (or Miss Taylor as we knew her) was a lovely Irish lady who helped look after the children who were boarding and was a bit like a matron. But she also had an office so may have been a sort-of housekeeper as well? I can remember that she returned to Ireland when she retired and was living near Kilarney - we visited her when we went on a holiday to Ireland not long after she went back there.

The school closed down in 1968. I think the Folliotts continued to live there for a few years but after Mr Folliott died Mrs Folliott moved to a flat in Keynsham.

From Katharine
Miss Taylor was a matron figure. She had a room on the top floor where I remember sleeping on the odd occasion we stayed. Mr Folliott ran the Vermipeat business from The Lons and I spent a few weeks in the office there in 1967/8. It was such a large house they may have had all sorts staying there after the school closed. Mr. F's mother was being looked after there at one time. I think she was bedridden. When the school was open there were some younger teachers who might have been there as live-in help.

The Lons as a School by Caroline Martin née Withers
I started school at the Lons in 1961 as a 4 year old. It was a mixed class of probably 10-12 children. My best friends were Irving Carter, a farmer's son from Dyrham (age 7 went to King Edwards). I remember him sewing his finger to a tapestry that we had to do on purpose I was impressed! My other friend was Jillian Gunter from Keynsham, we were later big Monopoly competitors. Other friends were the Perrett girls and the Richards girls also Alison Dobson-Smythe from Pucklechurch who used to ride home on her pony occasionally.

I often caught the bus to the Lons from Swineford and Miss Catling who was a very stern teacher (whose mother had been housekeeper to Sir Winston Churchill) used to walk me to the Lons if I hadn't missed the bus! She wore spectacularly jazzy glasses!

The picture on the left is Miss Catling's class in 1966 - so that is the top three years together. I am at the back on the right, Anne is next to me and Emma Richards is next to her.
Middle row far left is Caroline Withers. Anne Richards is in the front row second left.

Photo courtesy of Sarah Perrett

We had a very structured and varied education from Art history (still have the brilliant reference texts we were given) to needlework, history, bible study, ballet lessons, swimming (by dormobile to Hotwells in Bristol), nature lessons/ walks and needlework and Art besides the usual Maths and Geography and English. It was excellent and of course the super grounds to run around in. Mrs Folliott was an excellent head and produced amazing end of year theatrical productions and I still have many beautifully made costumes in our dressing up box.

Her husband was away a lot as a coffee grower I believe. Some children boarded. I had a friend called Gina from the Virgin Isles at the PNEU. The house was perfect I can picture it now with the green baize door separating private quarters of Mrs Folliott and the school area, the beautiful staircase and rooms in the top of the house. I left the Lons in 1967 or 1968 to go to Clifton High School.

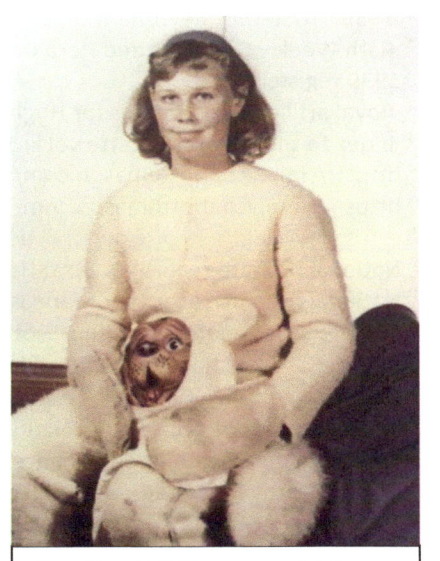

Caroline Withers, aged 10, playing Nana in a production of Peter Pan at The Lons.
Photo courtesy of Caroline

[1] Talking to my Five Children – Frances Folliott by Julia Scott
[2] Journal of Keynsham and Saltford History Society series 2 no 5 2005 gives a date of 1951
[3] The Folliotts first appear on the electoral roll for The Lons in 1955
[4] 1911 census for 94, Darenth road, Stamford Hill, Hackney, London
[5] 1901 census for Hackney
[6] 1911 census for Hugh Butler Folliott
[7] Electoral roll for 1932 and 1933
[8] Electoral roll for Hornsey 1933
[9] Marriage certificate for Hugh Butler Folliott and Frances Carlile Hale
[10] Talking to my Five Children – Frances Folliott by Julia Scott
[11] Queensland Births for Frances Carlile Hale to Herbert Percy Hale and Marie Isabel Carlile Thomas
[12] Oxford University matriculation lists 1891
[13] Clergy list 1896
[14] Inward passenger record for ship Ophir to Australia
[15] New South Wales Marriages 1909
[16] First World War Army Service Record
[17] Derbyshire Church of England births and baptisms for Hartington
[18] Talking to my Five Children – Frances Folliott by Julia Scott
[19] 1939 register for Keynsham
[20] Bath Weekly Chronicle and Herald Saturday April 2nd 1938
[21] 1939 register
[22] Royal artillery attestations for Hugh Butler Folliott
[23] Index to the London Gazette vol iii 1940
[24] https://simplycharlottemason.com/what-is-the-charlotte-mason-method/ accessed 21st November 2020
[25] https://simplycharlottemason.com/what-is-the-charlotte-mason-method/ accessed 21st November 2020
[26] https://fairfield.school/?id=pneu accessed 21st November 2020
[27] National probate record for Revd Herbert Percy Hale
[28] National probate record for Marie Isabel Carlile Hale
[29] Letters from Freetown by Julia Scott
[30] Journal of Keynsham and Saltford History Society series 2 no 5 2005
[31] Talking to my Five Children – Frances Folliott by Julia Scott
[32] Electoral roll for Haringey and National Probate record for Ellen Butler Folliott
[33] Talking to my Five Children – Frances Folliott by Julia Scott
[34] Talking to my Five Children – Frances Folliott by Julia Scott
[35] Talking to my Five Children – Frances Folliott by Julia Scott
[36] Marriage certificate for Hugh Butler Folliott October 6th 1934
[37] 1939 register
[38] https://www.saltfordenvironmentgroup.org.uk/history/history005-20Cp3.html accessed 23rd November 2020
[39] Outward passenger list for P&O Ship Canton for 9th January 1958
[40] Outward passenger list for White Star Ship Britannic 22nd August 1946
[41] Outward passenger list for P&O Ship Canton on 18th November 1949
[42] New York State passenger and crew list for Seven Seas Airline for 21st June 1960
[43] Letters from Freetown by Julia Scott

[44] Letters from Freetown by Julia Scott
[45] New York State passenger and crew list for Aer Lingus for 9th July 1962
[46] https://www.saltfordenvironmentgroup.org.uk/history/history005-20Cp3.html accessed 23rd November 2020
[47] Talking to my Five Children – Frances Folliott by Julia Scott
[48] Bristol Evening Post March 1st 1967
[49] https://www.saltfordenvironmentgroup.org.uk/history/history005-20Cp3.html accessed 23rd November 2020 See also *Ups and Downs of an Interesting Life. The Memoirs of Capt. John Scott M.N. by Julia Scott*
[50] From conversation with Julia Scott
[51] From John's Memoirs edited by Julia Scott
[52] Wikipedia https://en.wikipedia.org/wiki/Gilbern accessed 25th November 2020

For Further Reading
Talking to my Five Children – Why we are as we are – Frances Folliott ed Julia Scott *(CreateSpace Independent Publishing Platform 12 Oct 2014)*
Tony Folliott – Thoughts on my early years, 1937-1957 by Julia Scott *(CreateSpace Independent Publishing Platform 8 Aug 2018)*
Julia's Life in Photos 1947-2002 by Julia Scott *(Independently published 20 May 2019)*
Tony's Memoirs of Malaysia and Indonesia by Julia Scott *(CreateSpace Independent Publishing Platform 28 Nov 2012)*
Letters From Freetown by Julia Scott *(CreateSpace Independent Publishing Platform 11 Nov 2017)*

All of the above are available from Amazon

Special thanks go to Julia Scott both for talking to us about her family so enthusiastically and for allowing use of photos and text from her books. Also to Louise Cawthra who fully supported Bitton Parish History Group in writing about her family.

Chapter 10 The Lons Country Club

We now move to the final stage of our investigation, which is somewhat different from those sections that precede it. We have not found any written accounts of the period when The Lons was a country club, and so we have as our resource fascinating recollections. This section contains some memories and photographs, some from newspapers. Protecting privacy was a major concern. It is our hope that these memories will trigger further recall from our readers.

Graham and Anne Miller were the next owners of The Lons, paying around £34,000.00, and although the date of purchase is unclear, the wife of Graham's former business partner puts it at 1974. The previous owner, Hugh Folliott died in 1969, and his family sold to the Millers.

Extension at The Lons, 1976. Photo courtesy of Kingswood Heritage Museum and South Glos. Gazette

Julia Scott, Hugh Folliott's daughter, remembers that her father applied unsuccessfully for permission to build houses at the Lons. He was disappointed as this would have been his pension. Graham's application was successful, and he built substantial homes on the site.

Anne Miller (nee Kembury) was the daughter of a well-to-do builder of Woodstock Park, Kingswood. She appears to have been business-minded, while Graham was the front man, with an outgoing, entrepreneurial personality ideally suited to welcoming members to the country club that they established at The Lons. The leisure pursuits on offer were swimming, squash, a nightclub, and a venue for receptions and wedding breakfasts.

The swimming pool was popular with members, although not without incident. Roger, a local resident, recalls how beer glasses soon gave way to plastic because of breakages round the pool when imbibers became exuberant. However, as this photograph shows, it was also a fun place for families!

We think that the Millers installed the swimming pool, but they certainly built the three squash courts. Roger Fowler, a former member of the squash league, recalls how he was playing squash when, on the evening of the 8th August 1976, Kingswood Grammar School (which became Kingsfield School and is now King's Oak Academy) burnt down. He and some friends were rather proud to be on the scene just before Speedwell Fire Brigade!

Swimming Pool reopens at The Lons 1975. Photo courtesy of Kingswood Heritage Museum and South Gloucestershire. Gazette

Proficient Squash Court members could choose to play in the league: you were allocated a box of five or six players. Every month the list went up of who played whom and it was each person's responsibility to contact the organizer to arrange a swap. When they grew up, Adam and Simon Miller, Graham and Anne's sons, joined. Adam went on to play in the Gloucester County league. Less ambitious casual members could book a court to play at a less competitive level. Graham was a keen Bristol Rovers supporter, and its players were members.

The Lons Country Club
BATH ROAD, BITTON, BRISTOL

WINING, DINING AND DANCING
Tuesday—Saturday

CABARET
Thursday, Friday and Saturday

HIGH CLASS ENGLISH & CONTINENTAL CUISINE

Wedding Receptions and Parties catered for

Special terms for charity functions

TABLE RESERVATIONS—Telephone Bitton 3703

TEMPORARY MEMBERSHIP—48 hrs. notice.

ADVERT 1974

Photo courtesy of David Noble

The Lons nightclub was another attraction, mainly for members of the squash club, and on a good night would attract between 60 and 80 people. Every Saturday evening DJ John Kenway, assisted by his wife Sue, would play requests: Gladys Knight and Arthur Connelly were favourites of Roger and his wife Carole. She worked as a receptionist at The Lons, taking bookings for the nightclub and for wedding receptions.

Graham did the catering for receptions, with help from Neil Harding, who now owns a restaurant in Sidmouth. Keith and Doreen, his parents, ran Hardings TV shop in Fishponds. They were friends of Roger and Carole Fowler, with whom they used to meet up socially at the Lons while Neil was doing the cooking.

You may recognise Rev Poarch in this photograph taken in 1982, the year of the Falklands War. It shows him at the wedding reception of Barbara Merritt's sister, Clare and her husband John.

Photo courtesy of Barbara Merritt

The photographs below give an idea of the variety of social, charity and other activities that took place during this period. Hopefully, many will recognise family or friends.

Conservative Wine and Cheese at The Lons, 1976: photo courtesy Kingswood Heritage Museum and South Gloucestershire Gazette

Dinner for some people with disabilities at The Lons, 1981: photo courtesy Kingswood Heritage Museum and South Gloucestershire Gazette

However social activities at The Lons also strayed into more political ones. The photograph below shows the local MP, Jack Aspinwall, and others protesting against what they regarded as an unreasonably high rates rise imposed by Avon County Council. The rates rise was debated in Parliament and further protests across the country led to the Rates Act of 1984, allowing Parliament to cap increases.[1] In 1989 rates were abolished and the Poll Tax Community Charge was introduced, to similar acclaim!

1981 Rates demand and bonfire at The Lons. Photo courtesy Kingswood Heritage Museum and South Gloucestershire Gazette

Meanwhile, the Millers lived in a flat at The Lons with their three young children, Louise, Simon and Adam. In common with a number of local Warmley businessmen, they owned a holiday home in Portugal, which they frequently visited. Graham had a pilot's licence and owned a helicopter, which he would land at The Lons. He had an arrangement with the airline flying out of Bristol that Anne could sit in the co-pilot's seat whenever she wanted to return to Bristol. She was often unwell, and preferred at these times to go home. After her death, Graham returned to Bristol, sold up and lived on a barge in the harbour. The house itself was later converted to flats and these are largely unchanged today.

The Lons is still home to families, and so its history continues. Our MP resided there, as does our own Olympic medalist. Their lives, and those of others may perhaps encourage future generations to research the ongoing history of The Lons.

[1] For a full discussion of the debate in Hansard see
https://hansard.parliament.uk/commons/1981-07-23/debates/2dea18ea-79cf-458d-b494-a29eb3062275/Adjournment(RoyalWeddingAndSummer) accessed 1st January 2021

Information sources
Roger and Carole Fowler
Christine Radford
Barbara Merritt
Bristol Stories.org/story/182 (schoolboys tell the story of the fire)
Julia Scott
South Gloucestershire Gazette and Kingswood Heritage Museum